There's no deadline —
read this at your leisure.

Love,
Stephen
&
Carey

Christmas 1997

Tape for the
Turn of the Year

Also by A. R. Ammons

Ommateum
Expressions of Sea Level
Corsons Inlet
Northfield Poems
Selected Poems
Uplands
Briefings
Collected Poems: 1951–1971
(winner of the National Book Award for Poetry, 1973)
Sphere: The Form of a Motion
(winner of the 1973–1974 Bollingen Prize in Poetry)
Diversifications
The Snow Poems
Highgate Road
The Selected Poems: 1951–1977
Selected Longer Poems
A Coast of Trees
(winner of the National Book Critics Circle Award for Poetry, 1981)
Worldly Hopes
Lake Effect Country
The Selected Poems: Expanded Edition
Sumerian Vistas
The Really Short Poems
Garbage

TAPE

for the

TURN

of the

YEAR

A. R. Ammons

W·W·NORTON & COMPANY
New York   London

ISBN 0-393-03553-0

W. W. Norton & Company, Inc.
500 Fifth Avenue, New York, N.Y. 10110
W. W. Norton & Company Ltd.
10 Coptic Street, London WC1A 1PU

1 2 3 4 5 6 7 8 9 0

for Josephine Jacobsen
and Elliott Coleman

Tape for the
Turn of the Year

6 Dec:

today I
decided to write
a long
  thin
  poem

     employing certain
classical considerations:
        this
part is called the pro-
logue: it has to do with
  the business of
  getting started:

  first the
  Muse
  must be acknowledged,
saluted, and implored:
I cannot
write
   without her help
   but when
her help comes it's
water from spring heights,
warmth and melting,
     stream
     inexhaustible:
I salute her, lady
of a hundred names—
  Inspiration
  Unconscious
  Apollo (on her man side)
  Parnassus (as her
      haunt)
Pierian spring (as
    the nature of her

                    going)
               Hippocrene
               Pegasus:
          most of all she's a
          woman, maybe
          a woman in us, who sets
          fire to us, gives us no
                    rest
                    till her
               will's done:

          because I've decided, the
          Muse willing,
          to do this foolish
                    long
                    thin
                    poem, I
          specially beg
          assistance:
          help me!
          a fool who
          plays with fool things:

          so fools and play
          can rise in the regard of
          the people,
          provide serious rest
          and sweet engagement
          to willing minds:

          and the Muse be manifest:

          I'm attracted to paper,
          visualize
          kitchen napkins
          scribbled
          with little masterpieces:
                    so
          it was natural for
          me (in the House &

2

Garden store one
night a couple weeks
ago) to contemplate
    this roll of
adding-machine tape, so
narrow, long,
unbroken, and to penetrate
    into some
    fool use for it: I
thought of the poem
then,
but not seriously: now,
two weeks
have gone by, and
    the Muse hasn't
rejected it,
seems caught up in the
    serious novelty:

I get weak in
the knees
(feel light in the head)
    when I look down
    and see
    how much footage is
tightly wound in that
roll: once started,
can I ever get
free
of the thing, get it in
and out of typewriter
and mind? one
rolled end, one
dangling, coiling end?

will the Muse fill it
up immediately and let me
loose? can my back
muscles last? my mind,

can it be
as long as
a tape
and unwind with it?

the Muse takes care of
that: I do what I
can:

may this song be plain as
day, exact and bright!
no moonlight to loosen
shrubs into
shapes that
never were: no dark
nights to dissolve
woods into one black
depthless dimension:
may this song leave
darkness alone, deal
with what
light can win into clarity:

clarity & simplicity!

no muffled talk, fragments
of phrases, linked
without logical links,
strung
together in obscurities
supposed to reflect
density: it's
a wall
to obscure emptiness, the
talk of a posing man who
must talk
but who has nothing to
say: let this song
make
complex things salient,

saliences clear, so
  there can be some
  understanding:

7 *Dec:*

today
I feel a bit different:
my prolog sounds phony &
posed:
  maybe
I betrayed
depth
by oversimplification,
a smugness,
unjustified sense of
security:
    last
    night I
    read
    about the
geologic times
of the Northwest, the
periodic eruptions into
lava plateaus,
forests grown, stabilized,
and drowned
between eruptions:
in the
last
10,000 years (a bit of
    time) the
glaciers have been
melting, some now unfed,
disconnected, lying dead

and dissolving in
high
valleys: how strange
we are here,
raw, new, how ephemeral our
        lives and cultures,
    how unrelated
    to the honing out of
    caves and canyons:
    the lands, floating, rise
and fall, unnoticed in the
                rapid
            turning over
        of generations:

we, rapids in a valley
that millennially sinks:

nothing's simple, but
should we add
verbal complexity?

is there a darkness
dark words should
imitate?

I mean to stay on the
crusty
hard-clear surface: tho
            congealed
it reflects the deep,
the fluid, hot motions
and intermotions where,
            after all, we
            do not live:

10,000 yrs

    Troy
    burned since then:

but the earth's been
"resting"—entering
a warm
cycle: the Sumerians
had not, that long ago,
compiled
their
holy bundle of
the elements of civil-
    ization, nor
had one city-state stolen
it from another:

ten thousand years: how
many Indians is that,
fishing the northern
coast, marrying, dying?
coming & going, they
left no permanent sign
    on the warming
    trend:

I hadn't meant
such a long prolog: it
doesn't seem
classical to go ahead
without a plan:

wonder what plan
the Indians had
10 M years ago: the
        thought defines
        our sphere:

why should a world be
bigger than what a man
can reach
and taste and strike &
    burn & hunt & hold?

                    bigger than

that is metaphysics which
tho entertaining
is inedible
and unsurrendering: what's

10,000 years to us,
blips on
radar screens?

in the blip is all
imperishable possibility:
not unity, not all—
but the full,
complete: we can
in moments have
that
but when we
surround mind & world
to say all
in a single word,
we kill advantage with
the cost of gain:
can't we break loose
and live?

I wish I had a great
story to tell: the
words then
could be quiet, as I'm
trying to make them now—
immersed in the play
of events: but
I can't tell a great
story: if I were
Odysseus, I couldn't
survive
pulling away from
Lestrygonia, 11 of

12 ships lost
with 11 crews: I couldn't
pull away with
the joy of one
escaped with his life:
I'd search myself pale
with
responsibility, tho I'd
be in the wrong: that
we can't predict what
our actions will lead to
absolves us, tho not
altogether: we're held
to right deeds
and best intentions:

my story is how
a man comes home
from haunted
lands and transformations:
        it is
        in a way
        a great story:
but it doesn't unwind
into sequence: it stands
still
and stirs
        in itself like
boiling water
or hole of maggots: foam
or crust
can rise and
        sweep away into
        event: but not
    much of that:
mostly inner resolutions,
countermotions
that may work themselves

out
into peace,
bring the man
home, to
acceptance of his place
                    and time,
responsibilities and
limitations: I mean
  nothing mythical—
Odysseus
wandering in a ghost-deep
background—I mean only
or as much as
restoration
which takes many forms &
meanings:

but the story, tho
                    contained,
unwinds on this roll
with time & event: grows
like a tapeworm, segment
by
segment: turns
    stream corners: issues
in low
silence
   like a snake
   from its burrow: but
unwinding and unwound, it
coils again on
the floor
into the unity of its
        conflicts:

8 Dec:

the way I could tell
today
that yesterday is dead
is that
the little gray bird
that sat
    in the empty
    tree
yesterday is gone:
yesterday and
bird are gone:
I know there's no use
to look
for either of them, bird
running from winter,
yesterday
running downstream
to some ocean-pocket of
rest
whence it may sometime
come again (changed), new
as tomorrow:
how like a gift
the memory
of bird and empty tree!
how
precious
since we may not have
that configuration
again:
today is full of things,
so many,
how can they be managed,
received and loved
in their passing?

11

            on the bridle path
this morning
yellow horse-turds
glistened
with the moisture of
intestines:
a purple leaf occupied a
bush—a dozen kinds of
lichen on an oak:
eelgrass stood straight
up
on underwater banks:
someone told an
elephant joke: how do
you kill a blue elephant?
       with a
blue-elephant gun: how
do you kill a white
elephant? with a
white-elephant gun? no,
you tie a string around
his trunk and when it
turns blue
you shoot him with a
blue-elephant gun:
a little boy said, "Up,
up," begging to ride his
daddy's shoulders, and the
morning was warm and
       winter-bright:
from completeness
should one turn away?
so they drank wine
       and ate meat
and slept:
the shores fled

under the wind's weight:

why does an elephant lie
on his back? to trip the
        birds:

tonight, so
     compressed is
     chànge,
     we're having
warm weather and windy
rain: the house, however,
smells of
     fruitcakes baking and
merriment curls along the
ceiling,
giggles down the walls,
and tickles the floor:

the inexhaustible
multiplicity & possibility
of the surface: while the
depths are
     generalized into a
     few
     soluble drives,
interesting, but to be
        returned from:

the crust keeps us: the
volcano-mind
emits
this ribbon of speech,
smoke & heat
that held
would bust the cone off,
inundate the house
with direct melt:

but let off, there's
easing, mind cool, the
slow accretion of hard
rock:
doesn't matter how much
the core shifts
long as we have these
islands to live on: we're
in a
solid, hard, exact world
that tells all we
need to know of depth:

art casts into being, the
glow-wobbling metal
    struck by a
    difference of ice:

both necessary:
without flow, there's no
resource for crust:
without ice,
no sharp steel:
death is life's
    prerequisite:

this is that & that is this
& on and on: why can't
every thing be just itself?
what's the use of the
vast mental burden
of correspondence? doesn't
contribute to the things
resembled:

except in the mind: except
in the mind: there's
the reality that needs to

hold:

9:35 pm: lightning! what,
in December? just flashed
   blue-bright and
   thunder, moving slowly
and rumbling hard into
deep bursting depressions,
went all the way out over
the Atlantic: now, will
   the ground, shaken
loose, turn green,
loam to new roots?
the old people say it's
a use
of thunder: but this time
of year, the seeds asleep,
thunder's sterile
disturbance runs dreams
through the meat of the
future, a prophecy: no,
fancy,
never satisfied with
wonderless things as
they are: it's the
return of air upon
itself, following an
electrical discharge and
separation: the grass
seeds, hanging
in clumps on soaked stalks,
paid no attn &
thought of nothing:

 wind and rain have
 stopped: the
 thunder was a gigantic

period, punched over &
over: or do I hear now
a submissive, unwilling
drizzle?

sequence: events
stalled in their
occurrence: a
running with, fleet
recorder at the crest of
change: a plane is in
this: it rumbles in the
distance, a chord through
my circular knowledge: it
is out in the rain:

9 Dec:

sunny again:

last night a plane
over Delaware struck the
storm
& 80 lives descended in
flames: it's

the nature of flame to
rise, celebrant, spirit
to whirl upward:

80

111111111111111111111111
111111111111111111111111
111111111111111111111111
11111111111

    and he plucked two men

and broke fast

grieved, we
rejoice
as a man rejoices saved
   from death: we beg
that men be spared
calamity & the hard turn:
we make an offering of our
praise: we reaccept:

   our choice is
            gladness:

give us an idea!
let us be sorted out and
   assembled: let a new
order occur
from the random &
   nondescript:

let thoughts & emotions
fall behind into rank: or

return us from all idea to
undifferentiated
sensation—paradise:

1 pm:

had the storm last night
come half a mile farther
east, it would have
taken my roof off and
wet my poem
            (and my pants): it

"had a little twister in
   it," the man at the
Esso station said, came
right up the parkway,
took off

his plate-glass windows,
shattered the
outdoor movie's tall
wooden marquee,
    took the roof off
the concession and off
the Circle Diner and
  busted a window in
Kinney's: "must have been
a sucker," he said, "lifted
oil cans right off the
shelves"

reality last night was
more than I apprehended:
is far more today
than feebleness lets me
know:
wind ruined several dead
weeds and rain
de-seeded a lot of grass:

the cloud patterns
must have been fine,
dark roils
hidden by rain:

I wonder what all did
        happen? but
  the record
can't reproduce event:
even if I could know &
describe every event, my
account would
  consume the tape & run
on for miles into air:

those who rely on facts

have not heard:

those who rely on
arrangements—are
sometimes unwilling
        to surrender them:

those who rely on any shore
foolishly haven't faced
it that
only the stream is
                reliable: get
        right up next to the
break between
what-is-to-be and
        what-has-been and
dance like a bubble
held underwater by water's
pouring in: when the grass
moves on the hill,
it's impossible to tell
whether it has moved or
        will move:

my "mind" is trying to
keep every cell
        in my body
happy: yes, it says, we
understand that you need
so-and-so but we're
        temporarily (we hope)
out of that and are having
a substitute manufactured—
this will be released to
        you as soon as
possible: be sure to alert
your receiving dept: it
gets an alarm from a group

of injured or invaded cells:
we are
sending several divisions
   & several kinds of
   divisions to help you:
and so on:
catalysts, enzymes &
membranes, functions,
trades & forces, the
in-coming, out-going:
this mind that I turn
outwardly—how thin by
            comparison—
the body releases from
inner concerns and
gives few commands: get
food, water, sex: then
reality brings its
interference in
and the simple outward
mind, complicated by
postponements, symbols,
   prerequisites, proofs,
   nearly loses in
metaphysics &
   speculations its
contact with the
original commands: get
food, water: sex
is put upon you as the lust
of generations:
      it has been made to
      seem pleasurable
but is subservience
to the cry of flesh to
      endure: the inner
mind says—do that for

the cells, for us, and we
will free you to the
      pleasures of the
      outer mind:

get food, get water: sex
is a fire we send you:
quench it into
                  generations:
be brought low of the fire:

I've
given up hope of
      understanding for
what good is
understanding?
            understanding
what?

the conversion of
            currencies:
the multiplication tables:
IQ:
quantum theory & baby's
      formula
and how to replace the
shingles & whether to put
the money in SKF or
Xerox, and the clauses in
insurance plans &
   the "political
            situation":

plenty of food & water in
paradise but some
   confusion about sex:
anything so sweet
should come hard
as bread & water: so

they were given the
          gate: and
Eden survives in the mind
as half a solution:

analyze and project:
experience teaches
but stands to be
taught:

4:50 pm: the checker at
     the A & P said
he was returning from
Philly about 9:15 last night
and saw it: said the sky
     lit up,
he didn't know why
till the radio sd later:
said it wasn't hit by no
     lightning: said
     they have things
hanging from the wings:
said
he thinks it was
     turbulence, wind
turbulence—can take a
plane apart: woman
said
she's been up there & it
"gives her a funny feeling":

     one night I saw
something come apart
over Vineland: it
streaked in, glowed, &
     slowly tore apart:
I thought it was a
          satellite
               re-entering:

but next day read in the
papers it was seen from
Virginia to Connecticut:
        too big to land, as
        I thght it wd
        in Millville: was no
small potatoes:
first there was this blue
flash:

        here are "motions"
that play in and out:
    unifying
correspondences that
suggest we can approach
unity only by the loss
        of things—
a loss we're unwilling
to take—
since the gain of unity
  would be a vision
of something in the
continuum of nothingness:
we already have things:
    why fool around:
    beer, milk,
mushroom cream sauce,
eggs, books, bags,
telephones & rugs:
  pleasure to perceive
correspondences, facts
that experience is
holding together, that
what mind grew out of
is also holding together:
otherwise? how could we
perceive similarities?
                but all

the way to unity is
too far off: we have
a place:

at dusk a deep blue
sweeping smooth
cloud mass went just
between us
     and the ocean:
     but the night is
clear and full of stars:

10 Dec:

    sunshine & shade
     alternate at 32: winter
seems about to, but hasn't
quite decided how to
       happen:
(ideas give direction
but sometimes the wrong ...)

when the first
     horizontal haze of
sunlight struck the sumac
thicket this morning,
    bluejay flew in
    and sat on an outside
limb, his
appreciation, meditative
but imperfect, troubled
    by starlings:
    no place to stop:
the pure moment

self-centered & posed:

I heard of a little girl
  who wrote not
      "poems," but
"feelings"—some tissue
resulting from
things & feelings
at interplay:
to make a world
we need out of the reality
that is
and is indifferent:

    but play
removing us—we must be
  careful—a point away
  from reality, though
  an uncreated, unspecific
reality—that is, in a
sense, no reality at all:
what *is* out there? beyond
the touch of what
  we make?
whatever,
    stars shine through it
& bring us up
short:
we make a context
that lets us out, permits
fullest life: we must
care for ourselves,
    assume that, beyond,
we are cared for:

rely on feeling—
till it goes too far:
      then

on sweet reason which
recalls, restores, and
levels off: we must all
die, it's quite
     remarkable—
nevertheless, true:
but breakfast, and getting
off to school & work, and
what color to paint the
   second bedroom is
   meaningful: it's
            no
            great
joy to me
that I plunge deeply
(I think) into things:
eternal
significance is of some
  significance to me: I
don't know just how: but
temporal significance is
a world I can partly make,
loss & gain:

the social order obtains
identity
at the cost of certain
exclusions: unity
by the elimination of
difference: the pleasure
of the order is shared by
many, but the cost
   falls on a few: should
the many
be denied to relieve
the suffering of the few?
should the few pay
and not enjoy?

             if it's the few
who, alive to suffering,
advance the mind, do they
have their reward? and
the callous many? is
smugness the cost of their
        pleasure?
motions of
      society & psyche: what's
to be done?
ever been done?
greater tolerance of random
    without obliterating
identity?
relieve the suffering of
   the few & enrich the
many with difference?
if the oppressed are
freed, will they become
    callous
    and unfruitful?
will you have the secure
few and the oppressed
        many?
is freedom
identity without
            identity?

who's not working, slashing,
sweating, devising,
cheating to
    surpass the many and
rise into
the Few: (only a few
    who pride
themselves on being the
    Bottom Few?): is the
fight for the Top

the true mystique? first dibs
on food & sex:

               I know you,
man:
     am grateful to the
order, however imperfect,
that restrains you,
   fierce, avaricious: the
Top: Olympus,
the White House, the Register:
many lesser peaks in the
range: choose one and
   fight:
that's equality: if
inequality, must
   be a few hills even
   there:

what's the way home?
home?
what's wrong with these
deserts, excitements, shows:
excursions:

home is every minute,
occurring? just like this?

man, you're sweet &
          gentle to
          those who are
          no
          threat to your
          mt

          but are
          evidences that
          you occupy one:

I have your #: it's

me first after you:

Odysseus screwed a lot but
never got screwed: or
if he did, he screwed back
   harder, first
   chance he got: he never

"took nothing lying down":

my song's now
long enough to screw a
right good-sized article
with:
flexible to vault me
to the Top:
I hope it will lift me into
   your affections:
   that's what I need:
   the top I've chosen,
   the mt I wd climb:

the nest I've pro-
               vided
               for this
   song to wind into is
the wastebasket: that's
symbolic: the roll, tho,
   unwinds from the
   glazed bottom of an
   ashtray: I don't
      know what to make
      of that:
      phoenix?

why always
make something out of
         everything?
         maybe this song

will be about getting
home
and figuring out some
excuse to leave again:
that wd be gd bth cmng &
gng:

the clouds, continuous,
are creased with light
between furrows: like a
forehead, opposite with
shadow:

just sat down
to smoke, and the sun cast
my hand against the
wall, and my cigarette,
plus the lively shadow of
cigarette smoke:
that vast, immediate, hot
body
touching me:
     the sustaining
     chemistries that
separate it from me:
plankton, grass, pears,
apples, cows: steaks
holding heat,
the vessels of heat;
lambchops, chickenwings,

green peas, mushrooms,
cornflakes, coffee, pecans,
storers & storages of
heat: the warmth
     on my hand,
inside my hand: I
wonder
I don't

think about it more often:
transfigurations, touch:
  touches
everything and leaves a
shadow: kelp & birds &
pebbles even & each
individual blade of grass
& outhouses & mountains &
dead trees: even clear
water, toward the bottom,
accumulates some shadow:
     intimate,
     necessary
     & hardly ever
     mentioned: often
complained of, "the
  sun's in my eyes":
this burning while imprtnt
theories are discussed &
business goes forward:
"goods were shipped
last Thurs via PP"
ASAP, CIF, & FAS: & the
   lemon industry:
the sun, riding a moment-
to-moment crest: I
  hope it will keep on
riding: it's not a
     fixture:

noticed how
some nights the stars
are raw & brand new?
     make you feel
     slightly
     uneasy?
     it's the size
     & distance

unwinds you,
pulls you out
attenuating you
into
nothingness
till you grasp
around
at star-straws:

anybody doesn't believe in
reality should
try to start a dead car
on a 10-degree
morning:

maximum definition of
                        detail along
with
assumptions of symmetry:

I feel ideas—as forms of
beauty: I describe
            the form as
you describe a pear's
shape:
            not idea as ideal—
ideas are human products,
      temporal & full of
      process:
      but
idea as perception of form,
outside form that
      corresponds
to inner form, & inner to
outer:

(chaos at the bottom of
things & mind: only ideas
lift up from

there: only
groupings, saliences
of similarity &
   difference, only
clustering rises into
intelligence—instinct
itself an ordering,
overcoming great odds:)

a few flies are still
hanging around
the front porch:
   they're big blue:
   when the door opens
   they stir
   in the sun:
they remember or
still have the scent
   of the cat that was
   rotting behind my
   blue spruce: it's
   been below freezing
I don't know how many
nights: I thought that
was supposed to lay them
         but it ain't laid'em
         yit:
looks like it ain't
agonna: we can
know only so much & even
explanations
that hang round long as
flies
   have a way of going off:
   one of these days
a snow's crusty freeze
will draw'em a line
fiercer

than cat scent:
        catch them
napping at night
under leaves: turn
into some nap: long,
rich, bluegreen
        dreams:
beautiful, healthy-
looking flies, ate good,
long as the cat lasted:
had their day in
        the sunny nooks
        with lovely buzzes:

11 Dec:

they changed the forecast
today from
partly sunny to
mostly cloudy: not by
        prophecy:
        stuck their
heads out the window &
tho the instruments
didn't agree reduced
the gap between
prophecy & existent fact:
the direct
yields abundance, while
calculation
drags upon the event:

I beg that my eyes that are
open
be opened, that the

drives, motions,
intellections, symbologies,
myths—lift,
                     expose me
to direct
sight: seeing, I
color, alter, hide, accent:
but what is there, naked
    & nonhuman?
or here, deep &
terrifyingly human?
are we confined in an atom
with fiery nucleus? is
there too much room,
the ego under threat of
    dispersion?

you—who are you? how do
I feel about you?
do I hate it that I love
to be tied to you by love?
    untied, wd I be free
    or lost?

but for
your own sake: who
                     are you?
can I help? is there any
thing I can do:
are things
working out
all right for you? what
are those black areas?
are they parts
        of you that can't
        fall into place,
    come into light?
    are they longings &

fears only dreams whisper?

  I love you the best
    I know how:
    encounter me with
belief:

are you getting yours?
    getting & giving
yours, mine, & ours,
are we resolving most of
the areas, are we touching
      on elation
      enough?
do I love you mostly, or
the thought of us
          together?

are you hoping that
giving will make up for
not getting? that wd
be the course of saints:
      get, too: get it
      from me: I have it
      and having
      it for you, I get mine:

who are you, deeper?
have I sounded you? was
that
bottom I struck? but oh
up in the heart & around
your breasts
      and to speak of the deep
      in your eyes, have
      I come into your
         measure? are
you getting yours? have
you been had?

you've had me: I float:
   every cell
   comes to this:
             you are
beautiful: you are
just beautiful:
beautiful: thank you:

11:16 a.m: a blur of light
      just came into
the room,
lived a few seconds, then
died away:
my crown-of-thorns,
waiting, got the benefit,
struck across the middle:
      the instruments were
      right in a way:
emphasis distinguishes
partly sunny from mostly
cloudy: if it don't
      snow it's gonna miss
      a good chancet: I'll
say that:
lagging behind the event:
running to catch up: to
      be at the
      'crest's break, the
      running crest,
event becoming word:

anti-art & non-classical:
in art, we do not run
to keep up with random
moments, we select
& create
the moment
occurring forever:

timelessness held
at the peak of time:
(just went to take a leak:
jay on the back lawn,
hopping, looking around,
turning leaves)

but this may turn back on
itself, motion by motion,
a continuum, held in
timelessness
racing with time,,,,like
a napkin
burnt in the ashtray, red
beads, flameless, racing
around, splitting, dying,
turning fiber into ash:
held activity: —

let's have faith to go
ahead & see if anything
will happen:
maybe the tape will run out:

(looks a long way off:
Muse! Muse! fiery
woman, what
you got to tell me?
tell me:
I feel weak so
much tape remains:
my back's getting sore:
I don't sleep good
with this going on—slept
pretty good last night:
woke up once
into a country of dreams:
wanted to remember them:
but mostly cloudy was

too bright, even,
for them: it *was*
a country, I think: great
many people: & no news
of my book at the pstffce
again this morn: so I
don't feel
strong about
things: I
need plenty of help:
the crusty world
takes no notice:
Muse, what must we
do to hit the top:
it'd better
be good: give a little,
will you, please?) (I'm
bushed:)
but you can do worse
than be a singer of verses:

(I'm the biggest
fool that ever was—
assertion's not the
way to the top, you're
a little round fool—
to follow you off into
these woods: who are you
anyhow? some kind of a
prickteaser?)

& so & so & so &
so & so
&
so & so & so & so so

(some kinuva sans merci?)

lunch: hot dogs and baked

beans again: swell:
2/23: 11½¢ a can: cheap:
hotdogs run you around—
  oh let's see:
this morning's coffee &
a chocolate fudge cookie:
maybe 30¢ altogether:
& all
that energy
turned into verse
will bring
you
about
four condemnations:

    transformations!
      metamorphoses!
        mitachondria!
          hell's bells!

how my back hurts: even
by concentrating, I can't
feel any presence
to my balls: missing:

wd it be masturbatory if
I if I
  touched the area
briefly
just to make sure?

two cool tight weights!
    thank you:
thank you very much:

if I had a flute: wdn't
if be fine
to see this long thin
poem
rise out of the waste-

                    basket:
the charmed erection,
stiffening, uncoiling?

anyways, that wastebasket
is coiled full: wonder if
I should stomp
            in it?

in & out: weaving in &
              out: a
tapestry, looking for all
the world
as if it were alive:

(break we that watch up)
just took a ride out
to the refuge: 100,000
birds: mallards, grebes,
teals, herons, Canada
                geese &
two excellent flyers
    from which there is
        no refuge:
one, the short-necked,
long-tailed red hawk: he
browses the marshes &
for the little bird,
little bird
he is carefully looking:
& way overhead, turning,
the quiet, black
vulture:
two avenues flesh
can take: the tight red
& the loose dark meat:
        red ambulance
        & black hearse,
brazen reminders: and the

birds fly among, regarding
& regardless:

the trash collectors came
while I was gone &
         took the
week's waste away: we
     are purged: even
a house has the incoming &
outgoing energies
& losses by which it
     is maintained:
the garbage truck
says on the back
     "We aim to serve,
          not disturb":
sophisticated
assonance

          & & & & & &

intellections are
     scaffolds, trellises
we wish some vine of
          feeling would take to
& possess
completely:
          spider build
          a circle
hung in
the squares of: bird
light on & sing from
the top of:
     we build them even
for the windsong's
tenuous life:
chance
     a vine will ramble up it
busting into leaves & roses,

42

giving the robin a place
& making all the air
   around
   fragrant: we build these
structures because we
have hope, at least:
          we're
   flat & lifeless,
   but these erections,
they have hollow spaces,
room: we mean
   to change—that is,
a sprouting is going
to go on: good, bad, &
indifferent are gonna
clutter up all around,
   rise through the
   lattices
   of held space
   and sing all
together, rose,
   thorn,
   smear of birdshit:
   gonna rise
right up out of the
          ground
where the dreams wait
and be red & gold
and laughing to beat the
          band:

intellections are
bowls we hope to fill:
motions on the
prowl:
don't
cut them
down or bust them up so

43

the water spills
& the vine hunts
aimlessly over the ground:

do
not be impatient with us:
we're coming along &
        meantime
entertain yourselves with
the dry beauty of our
    joists & timbers, slats
& designs:
if nothing ever breaks
into leaf
still we
meant to encourage
        the vine: we like
        the call of the
robin & his early visit &
the color of his hen's
eggs &
the way he stands on the
        lawn, erect—
    dressed for a wedding:

intellections have a use,
don't think they don't:
if the vine couldn't
find a natural tree, what
    would become of it? if
structure without life is
meaningless, so is
    life without structure:
we're going to make a
dense, tangled trellis so
    lovely & complicated that
every kind of variety will
find a place in it or on

44

it: you just be
        surprised: &
        forgive us:
        who mean song
    direct & fierce:

(this day
  ended
    in spite of all
      mostly sunny)

a dark night of stars
ensuing:

help me:
I have this &
        no other comfort:
        the song,
the slight, inner
unmistakable song you
give me
and nothing else! what
        are you,
some kind of strumpet?
will you pull out on me?
look: I have faith: I
have faith: come or go:
I'll always love you:
I have nothing else:
I have
nothing else besides you:
will you tear me
        to pieces? I'll go
on without you, until
you come again:
                    then
      in the flare of song

we'll make a common flame:

if it ain't one fantasy
it's anothern: where
  are you, reality?
  come out of there:
you drift around in the
background, drooping
like a suckegg dog:
probably I'd like you
    all right
if I could get up close
enough to know you:
are you pieces of things
not quite fastened?
what's your face like?
        frowns &
        bitters?
        witchy?
        scrawny?
        warty?
        withery?
maybe I've given you a
horrible mask
and behind that you're
  beautiful: or
is this another dream,
reality's dream?
  then, is reality to be
free of fantasies, those
I hang between us,
  those I cast on you?

fact is, I'm having
this conversation with a
piece of paper!
  and "you" are a figment
of imagination and "you"

have no mask
& if you did
no face
wd be behind it:
all this is just coming
out of my head:
the factory of fantasies:
some beautiful, some
terrifying,
some this, some that—but
all, paper & thin air!
  a hundred dragons
and furies, satyrs &
centaurs—and one
Muse!
        get food:
        get water:
        get sex:
bank account, nice car,
good address, retirement
plan, investment portfolio,
country-club membership,
monogrammed shirts, summer
home, cabin cruiser, big
living room (furnished
modern)
        Money
        Power
        Food
        Water
        Sex—and who needs
paper conversations,
words revved up in a
fine motion and a headful
of dragons?

reality, I've got a feeling
you can be awful nice! but

if the only reality
I can get is a spare,
    hard-bought one, why
turn on the fantasies and
let there be gorgeousness,
color & motion,
red & gold fabrics
and fine illusioning silks!

the man with bills to pay
dreams with a Muse!

reality is
knowing what you want
and how
to get it:

12 Dec:

clouds came in soon after
dark last night, and today
broke fact & prophecy
as snow turning into rain:
    the starlings sit
    like rainsheds,
    vertical in the gray
trees: two jays
search the ground:
as
it neared midnight last
night, I felt
pulled to go out
and hunt the roosts of
birds, flush them & hear
the shrieks of panic,
    blind beating wings:

I wanted to know
what birds do at night,
how they
handle surprise, of
weasels, foxes, snakes:
I wanted to know
if they're adequate
to the night:
I wanted to hear them
settle down
as I turned away, feel
the sweet emptiness
of their panic:

yesterday at the refuge, I
saw a fingerling,
     crosswise
in a rising gull's beak,
shiver at both ends:

and last night, after
anger & a family tiff, I
suffered a loss & breakage
  of spirit, blankness
as of plateaus: my "poem"
turned to incontinent
prose, unburned by spirit,
and this occupation
    with a rolled
    strip of paper
blackened to
obsession, senseless,
slightly mad: the Muse
cleared out, leaving an
empty house:

but she's back with me
today, I think: I hear
a little voice

49

singing
under my brain, and I know
she's there,
     modest & faithful:

at the postoffice, no news:
nothing is out there
in the world: or it's
     all turned to concrete:
I've won no battles & lost
none:
     am engaging no
          realities:

cause enough to stop &
     tear: cause enough
to sleep today, rest my
back & brain: except
that song itself
     is enough, needs no
appeals beyond itself,
tightens fantasy
into matter
to outlast
this day's real concerns:

soundless mist,
     collecting, sounding
in the gutterspouts:
the saliva bed sucking in
my pipe, the moaning suck
of a dying bird:
the burry buzz of a
distant, peripheral plane:
the yellow, octagonal
pencil, rocking as I write:
the air & surface burn
of cars on Tilton Rd—heat
kicking on & off, baseboard

cracking, freezer
wheezing—silence,
broken by keys:

<pre>
          *
        ***
       *****
        ***
          *
</pre>

clusters!
organizations!

<pre>
       *****
       *****
       *****
</pre>

shapes!

)/(/(/)/)/(/(/)/)/(

designs!

close suspension of
cloud: not a break or
        beam: the jay
jumps around in the naked
sumac thicket, squalls,
complains, stares at a
        head of sumac-seed,
pecks it violently, as
with contempt: what a
jar, moist rattle: the
seed-head comes still
again, indifferent:
the crown-of-thorns has
had so little sun, the
four-flowered spike,
                opening, is
                pale pink
that in an outside

summer sun would be
   blood red:
not much green
on the walls of
the aquarium: the snails
   are sluggish (!)—

the sky is like
neon lighting, a
   ceiling of light
   without origin, no
   fierce disc
   radiant, recognizable
source: equal diffusion:
and when
the Florentines painted
radiant populations in
   the heavens, they were
         not wrong:
         each of
us,
says modern science, is
radiant,
       tho
       below the
       visible spectrum:
paradise will
refine our radiance
or give us better sight:
   we're fallen
   now:
   we may be raised into
   knowledge & light:
   lower would be
longer & longer wavelengths
to dark's undisturbed constant:
may we
not go there

but ever & ever up
    singing into shining
light:
but not too high:
there's a zone we
    do best in: beyond
    on either side, we
go by instruments
and artificial atmospheres:
a stark way:

we are, as bodies,
"localizations"
supported by barriers,
        holding in &
        shutting out:
systems of
exclusion, permitting
    certain inlets, outlets:
we are
"held together":
minerals—such as
            calcium—
    selected, refined
    & deposited to high
    purities
            give support:
specialized tissues
bind us to the bones: an
outer cage
protects softer organs:
            lovely
        loose mesenteries—
            permitting digestion's
            roil & change—
hold intestines in place:
    so
    the exchanges can go

on, the trades in
blood, lymph,
food, waste, water:
traffic through
barriers, each selective,
responsive:
if you have condemned the
body, you have
condemned a miraculous
residence—
temple
we should try to keep
the right spirit in:
the aggregates! the
widening accumulations,
providing the molecules,
proteins, triggers
we need:

imperfect, tho beautiful,
body: when it can
no longer defend, repair,
grow—when mineral
ash (that could not be
processed away) stiffens
the cell walls
so they lose flexibility
& effect—then the balance
turns
to invasion and
disintegration:

nothing permanent is old:
what is forever has no
youth or age: if you
could choose, how
wd you choose?

the biochemist, first

seeing how
two molecules select each
other & interlink
   must think he
   beholds
   a face of God:
& from the center of all
these balances,
   coordinations,
         allowances,
integrations—waves
register & float away into
nothingness: there is
      mind:
before you desecrate this
place, study its
architecture:
      but the mind doesn't
      insist we know all
      this: its commands
are few:
      reproduce this temple
      before it falls:
      food, water:

barriers!
what is it, exactly, that
exists
when I see fish
travel in water & birds
in air?
resemblance
   tying high above
   difference:
wings, fins: air, water:

13 Dec:

my book came today, Friday
    the 13th:
wooooooooooooooooooooooooo
wooo wooo woooooooooooooo

6:35 pm: we went
Christmas shopping at
    Korvette's and
    Cherry Hill:

had dinner just now
over to Somers Point at
Mac's: fried shrimp—
    & Phyllis had
crab:
they have a good salad
dressing there: don't
know what it is
    (on the
    order of French) but
they call it "Mac's":

bought Aristophanes's
complete plays, very
saxy (I hope)—I'd read
Frogs & *Clouds* (no, it ws
Birds) before:
    mostly, I walked
    around carrying my
    bk:

14 Dec:

    today
came in an

opposite way
of rain turning into snow:
when I woke up
the gutterspouts were
dripping musical flutes:
the tones dangled &
    broke &
ran together with
inexhaustible variety of
      mood & shape:
but now (10:50 a.m.) the
same colorless, closed sky
turns weight
     into fluff, fast pellets
into slow blurs
that touch rainpools with
many-fingered hiss
& melt into silence: &
    the grass seems
    to rise up &
    cushioning bring down
the flakes:
as if a god slept hereabouts
and meant to make a winter
   of his sleep:

(snow, a servant to
   Agathon, cloistered up
    with odes)

soft prisons are the
      worst kind: bars
      & stones are
      honest, exact,
but this insinuation,
insisting it's not itself,
this deepening
with universal touch: not

a path, road
left: only circles of
   melt-stain under naked
   trees (the flakes
       caught in a
       foliage to
       branches) as if
the roots
sent up a warmth of
protest
or stirred radiating
    summer dreams:

and (it's not very cold)
the foliage melts & hangs
rainbeads
   on twigs & branches—
points of clarity
concentrating light
    into sources:

no birds this
morning: they
fear these white bodies
that fly into a still
white starvation:

a few seed, hung on
weeds & grasses, fall
& pepper the snow:

the reason I write so much
is
that I can't do anything
else:
poem must be now
close to 40 feet long: I
can't get it out
to write letters or

postcards or anything:
    well
    if
    it
    must
    be
    onward
    to
    the
    end,
    let's
    get
    there
    in
    a
    hurry: or
is that cheating?
every time the roll turns
it speeds up: as the
diameter decreases, the
revolutions per foot (rpf)
increase, so the poem
should rise to a pitch of
unwinding
          at the end: a
spinning of diameter into
nothingness:

exclusions:
lepers on their islands,
drunks imprisoned in
    drunkenness,
the disappearances (un-
noticed—the streets
seem always full,
lively & young enough)
into illness, stiff bones,
strokes, graves:

the silent child that stays
indoors,
unable to connect:
I feel the bitterness of
fate: I feel the
bitterness of fate:

what it means to
drive away from the
      house: take a walk
      down the street:
      join the daylight
      world's clean going:

are we as innocent of our
      joy
as they are of their
        despair?

must do what we can,
   accept the rest:
      God, help us: help us:

we praise Your light:
give us light to do what
we can with darkness:

    courage
    to celebrate Your
    light
    even while the
    bitterdrink
    is being drunk:

    give us the will
    to love
    those
    who cannot love:

    a touch of the dark
    so we can know how one,

hungry for the light,
can
turn away:

we're here together:
is it known,
has it been determined
what is right to do?

give us a song
sanctified
by Your divinity
to make us new
& certain of the right:

should I sacrifice
myself for
others? would
they, alarmed,
turn in confusion
against me?

should I care for
myself only,
bring to its fullest
enunciation
what fate says in me?

we're here together,
though:
let us know when
to reach out &
when to withdraw:

& so & so
the snow has
turned to grit: I had
lunch after
"who cannot love"—
soup, sandwich, milk,

chocolate fudge cookie, &
coffee (my wife's home
         today)—most
         of the week she
         works,
         while I sit
         home in
         idleness:

I'm waiting to hear if
Cornell will give me
a job: I need
         to work &
         maybe I write
         too much:

silenced by
exclusion: we
don't hear the
         suffering: it
doesn't exist
and we are untroubled:

         prisons!
         constellations!
         shapes that possess
         &
         entangle the mind!

         run yourself through
         Beethoven's
         Sonata Pathétique &

         exist like a bush!
         willing entrapment
         of cell walls &
                  diamonds, a giving
of the self
over

into shape, structure
   played upon
   by motion & flesh!

   they say there are
   water molecules in the
         void—

   then it's not empty!—
motions racing
through, particles &
drifts, a structure
   woven
   beyond the
   diaphanous:

but here
around the roots of trees,
a black engendering:
prisons,
hold fast!

safe in these cages, I
sing joys
that never were
   in any thorough jungle:

but betimes & at times
let me out of here:
I will penetrate into the
void
& bring back
nothingness
to surround all these
        shapes with!

closing in
   without closing:
   running through
without filling:

opening out
    with walls:

run my poem through
        your life & it will
        exist in you
        like a protein
            molecule:

clothes to try on, wear,
abandon or keep:
put away in the closet,
        a memory ectoplasmic
with gone joys:

what am I doing?
what are my innermost
        feelings?
do I know what I'm doing
    or am I waiting
        for it to
            be done?

my innermost feeling is
a silky pouring of
        semen, a rich
disturbance
in the groin,
broken loose, flowing free:

I remember a stallion
had been stalled for wks:
in the lot surrounding
him were mules & mares:
        someone let down the
        gate &
        he hit the nearest
bony old mule and gave
her a rapt opening,
        invasion & filling,

64

& in a slick moment he
was shot: as if shot,
dropped to the ground
   and the loose wobbling
   weight
   poured & poured on the
   ground
& he came up & took her
again: she braced
herself and groaned:

the rich pouring
of this verbal
itch:

   I fall back:
   shot:
   winded:
   God, relieved, sweet
floating relief:

imprisoned in marvelous
desire
and set free! beautiful
bth gng in & cmng out:

the men, embarrassed,
joked & hid
their hard-ons against
      the fence: they

knew the stallion
stalled in the prison of
his honest lust: you,

find the exit,
 the wooly
    entry
and go free & take an
honest part

in the community: many
things to be
accounted for,
to take into account:

oh this poem is long:
the tape's still thick
& slow:
Muse, come & take my
riding, rouse my riding:
we got a long long way
    to go: present

    the cage men will
dwell in, design the
gleaming city:

cars hiss on the highway:
typewriter clicks:
    the thermostat snaps:
(sounds like a motorcycle
out there)
the day's unchanged—gray
undivided clouds:
but the
snow's stopped:

we went out after "& we
are untroubled" up there:
I unpacked my mother-in-law's
new dishes
& Phyllis helped wash them:

(forbidden, their is
forbidden suffering:
they turn inward & inward
calls hopelessly
to inward: song, poor

song, life them outward
if you can)

an object,
exactly perceived
& described is
when entered in the
              tapestry
somewhat compromised:
part strength flows
from it
to its
compositional environment:
no tapestry
without
this clustering,
giving up of strength:

no tapestry then! if it
impose what may
enter! forget it!

              but no exact
              thing, either,
              unless it
calls & calls away to
kindred things:

              the job is
              honest,
full as a suspected
reality
of tensions:. to keep
the object clear as
it can be (& itself),
the
tapestry "one" as it can
be,

without tyranny:

partial solutions: men
feared
at the end of the 19th
century
that they were going to
solve the universe: no
more need of physicists!

    just as the
    whole fell
    together it
    fell apart:

innocent again,
the physicists are
    re-employed:
(I'm glad somebody's
working:
wish I were making some
money myself)

       @

back off there, populace!
the poet will have a little
    room!
disburden the area: hey,
you: git off da stage!
    the poet will take
a little distance on:
what?
can you think these
    "private" things are
    private?
they were got from
jokes & dirty books:
the poet, lawsee, but
sings to the general

             & claims
but the murmur in the words:
have at you, sir!

the poor employee of the
ruling queen, the listener
to lies that
they may become truth:
the raiser of halcyons
into storm: the public
voice
that has no pleading of
its own: but, indeed,
bends to the great,
will take coins
      to th'amusement:
that will, cold as a
                    glass, give
the hag the hag,
the beauty beauty, the
evildoer his face:
to the courts with your
   disgraceful shows!
   here
   the poet lolls, suckled
up in the rapture of his
sacred saying:

a nerveless creature
      because all nerves:
odd-one-out
because he stands aside to
see: fool that makes
   foolishness a law:
will you be ruled,
sir, metered out?
the poet implores you to
get the hell off his back:

he will have
room
and a universe
to cry all day
the trampling of a weed:

go you the hell all on
back home: or stand off:
the music *descends:* look
up: there, now: there:
     thank you, gentlemen:

and goodnight: it's past
twelve and a
     cold, freezing, windy
          night:

                    %

15 Dec:

my poem went for a ride
today: I
          backgutted it all
the way out
of the typewriter,
rewinding the roll:
stuck it in a paper
bag, then in the
     glove compartment:
we all went to York, Pa.
to visit relatives:

I was reluctant to give
the day to myself & not
to the poem: but
     the thing I couldn't

do was separate us:
what if the house caught
fire while I was gone?
unh, unh: took it with me:

but mightn't you have had
a car accident & ruined it?
mebbe but bebbe I'd
have ruined myself, too,
        past caring about
        poems,
        mebbe:

took it with me: & have
returned (10 pm) &
reinserted & rewound:

I'm beat: drove
there & back & drove
a lot while there,
    looking the city over,
the place my nephew
goes to school & where his
    daddy works & shopping
centers, bowling alleys
& the ritzy section,
mansions way up
on the highest ridge—
overlooking:
        the Top:

but it's late:
excuse me, I'm tired: &
the cold drops—
they say to 5 or 10 above
tonight:

16 Dec:

first I heard
on the radio this morning
it was
19 degrees:
but it's bright sunny
and
believe it or not
   there're a couple of
flies
out on the porch, still
okay, doing fine
on "areas of warmth":
   but doing I don't
know what at night:
a one-legged starling
was hopping around on the
porch when I just drove
up: and a catbird was
    sitting
in the green-withered
rhododendron bush,
warming:

the joy of the crest,
riding & writing
in the going making
single stream: but I
   can't always live
   there:
obstructions:
frustrations:

frazzling reality,
   many-fingered &
   dividing: what

self-acceptance, strength
of self, is
needed to meet it:
the gain's in doing
little things: but

wherever you turn, someone
beat you there, is
in your way
obstructing you: some
        idiot pulls out
        in front of you,
without notice or
hesitation: someone pops
on his brakes: another
drags along:
somebody behind you blasts
his horn:

here, the obstructions
continue: the flow
lost, the crest gone: the
self not
pulling all together:

if things were easy
they'd be valueless:
wd they?
this is easiest when it
rides highest
& when it's difficult
nothing can be done:

this fantasy: with
faith, unity, I
may turn it into a
        pleasing reality:
wdn't that be a blast:
        wdn't that break up

73

pragmatism:

(there you go
  picturing yrself
  worldwide again: easy,
  boy: you
  dooky like
  everybody else)

it's a loss of love:
I love all those
people (provided
they get out of my way)

hostility, thrust, that
drives one to this
    thrashing of keys:
violence of vowels:

prisons of hostility,
gleaming as Manhattan
plate-glass towers:
solitude—so as not to
                strike!

death's
the maximum-security
prison: take a lot of
practice
to spring
that one: too secure:
turn our faces into
cold wind &
risk's hard fact:

I feel like running:
& wd:
except there's no
place to
run to: prisons to let

ourselves into
and out of:

>   what kind of mess
>   am I in today?
>   Muse, if you
>   want anything out
>   of me, you'll have
>   to do a little
>   fixing-up:

this tape is too damn long:
I'll tell you that:
terrible task:
>   then you go off & whore
>   around:

10 pm: we've just
finished addressing the
>   Xmas cards (policy:
send one to people
who sent one last year—
with some eliminations
(somebody has to make the
first move:) some additions):
>   stars, angels, snow,
donkeys, trees, bells, arches,
>   windows, children: not
a bad context, though
reality
has a
way
of
wandering around the edges
of
it: I'd take a liking to
it if it wasn't for
still having the stamps
to lick:

next yr I intend to send
a card to everybody
I know (I think)—
that's not a bad context &
it says a lot about peace:

just went to Tony's to
get a pack of cigs: it's
colder than you
can imagine: must be
around 8: yipe!

17 Dec:

Sisyphus
  struggling
   with his
      immortal
       rock: some say this
is all man's work,
crumbling castles, decay-
ing systems—absurdity:

but Sisyphus
knew each upward strain
& groan
soaked into the hard
potential of the stone,
that the sweat burned in
deep:

mountaintop, he released
weeks of energy
and saw—each time as
miracle—the
gravity-bound, difficult

rock
leap & lollop
like a deer,
feather-light, bird

awing: & he let out a
cry of joy that
rang through the
valley
mixing with stone-thunder:

the people—who'd
forgotten Sisyphus & his
breadless labor—screaming
jumped out of bed
& ran
out into the night:

Sisyphus took
light, jerky
steps downward
and resolving came,
luminous with explanation,
among the people:

they cheered &
thanked the gods
for the return of reason

& Sisyphus, the
groans all vented from
his rock
turned to the empty, easy
thing & rolled it like
a playball over the even
ground
up to the bottom of the
rise:
the people, smiling, went
to bed & through

the black morning hours
the rock,
breaking branches, began
to take on
again its difficult majesty:

¢¢

got
    to leave Sissy Fuss
    & go
    pick out the Christmas
    tree:
    keep it cold in
    garage: so it don't
turn stiff & sheddy:
    cut'em around October:
    why
    they cut'em so soon?
    transportation:
    it's merchandising:
dealerships to work out:
farmers to contact: red
        tape: whatd'ya
think?
they can just appear up
down here
fresh
two days before Christmas?
sheez!
some kindova nut:

        grows on a tree,
        a tree is part of
            Nature,
    Nature is beautiful &
    thank you for the

compliment:

why don't we go cut
our own?
cut our own!
where?
but we don't own that land:
whatd'ya mean they don't
care?
I know they're beautiful:
grow right up in the
fallow land,
    taper up nice, standing
out half-deep in
    Indian grass, right
out in the middle of
    the field:

when I was a boy:
or a bit more:
used to go get the
    Christmas tree: lived
way out in the country
down in Carolina
in a time
& place
that seem so long ago,
everything different
now & sort of loused up:

an only boy & I would get
the axe &
follow the paths over the
fields & back of the
    fields come into
hill-woods (hickory,
    lush-leaved tree,

covering the ground each
year with
thick-shelled nuts)
& then into the swamp woods:
    for
in the South
cedar grows deep
    in the damp swampwoods
and then it's sparse, so
sparse, where I come from:
& walk & walk, roaming and
nearly lost:
there's one! already
    topped: and found
another, shaggy, topped
years ago: & finally
finally finding one
        bushy, full, &
        pointed:
climbing and with that
awkward, ungrounded swing,
hacking away at the
        trunk:
dragging it home, the limbs
obliging, flowing with
the motion:

we had no electricity but
we had pinecones &
    colored paper &
    some tinsel: it
was beautiful enough:
it was very lovely:
& it's lost:

though there's no
    returning (and
shd be little desire

to return) still we shd
keep the threads looped
tightly with past years,
the fabric
taut
& continuous, past growing
into present so present
can point to future:

where am I now?
in a house with
no acres around it—don't
        even own an axe—
plenty of electricity but
no hickory nuts,
no rummaging the swamp
for the scented green,
the green-green, moist,
growing right on the tree:
now, a tree from
somewhere—maybe Vermont—
got by handing over
    two or three green
    pcs of paper:
        $$$$$$$$$$$$$$

do you hear me, Sisyphus,
durn you? do you hear me
groan:
 like:
  wow:

2:29 pm: (still sunny)

I better get out of
    here & go
    get that tree:
the good ones are

gonna be gone:

The little tree
on the hill
could surely be
bright & still

except the wind
round the hill
has a mind
that isn't still

&

I decided not to get the
tree:
instead, I lay down on the
couch
& nearly fell asleep
& then sat up
& then
the little tree
   came to me:

4:30 pm: the sun's sunk:
we approach the shallows
of the year: short
   days with the sun
   gone south:
   the light will
lengthen, break through
plate-glass ice,
stir roots & bees:

in a maze prison, you're
free: every wall
      opens:
you move around with
trial:
you know there's a way

82

out:

the mind turns & fails:
and turns & fails: loss
of bearings & origins:

the maze shrinks into the
head, paralyzing: unwind
it, un-
wind it!

speaking of memries,
I member
this little spring
that came mouthing out
of sand at the foot
of the pasture:
I dammed up a good-sized
pond around it,
black mud walls
maybe 6″ high:
        held the flow,
gave it structure:
still the little mouth
kept talking
in the clear pond: clear!
you could read the grain
in the bottom mud,
kind of fluffy:
frogs laid eggs in it:
messy eggs
with little black eyes:
beautiful & sticky:

they say the night will be
cold
with increasing cloudiness:

probably: snow tomorrow:
flurries:

18 Dec:

today
broke as if under water:
horizons & dome diffused
with completely
increased cloudiness:

a set of four thumb-size
birds
flicker in the sumac
grove:
the sun's a silver bead
behind the clouds:
flurries expected:

Christmas trees come
stout, stubby, tall, lean,
bunchy, lopsided, scrawny—
besides the kinds—cedar,
    pine, fir:
my wife & I diverge
    at scrawny-bunchy: she
likes bunchy ones (even a
    little stubby): I like
    scrawny, open trees:
like to get inside the
tree
and hang it full of
        ornaments:
        I
        don't
        like
those bunchy ones that
thrust you out, accept only
peripheral trim:

chacun à chacun, tho: that

is, the devil with it:
    husband & wife hold
    each other off
    by digging
chasms of difference:
then they have a hell of a
time bridging them: it's
important that a male be
different from a female—
the greater the difference
the higher the charge—
      but if the
difference gets too wide,
the two halves
drift off into alienations:

ever noticed how
dark it is
inside those bunchy trees?
they hover-in the
dark, withholding, secret,
mysterious:
what? have a system of
              darkness
standing in the living
room, recalcitrant,
impenetrable? the devil
take it!

      —or—

I cd think of it as
protected darkness,
    boundaried by
ornament & light:

maybe that's a deeper
response

than my fully exhausted

85

             open tree:

everybody to his own taste,
said the old man as
    he kissed the cow: (and
every little bit helps,
said the old lady as
    she peed in the ocean)

10:29 a.m: the bead's gone:

11:40 a.m: fine, hurrying snow:

12:48 pm: everything white:

3:20 pm: still snowing: I
        went to the
cleaner's, egg-lady's,
& mailbox & just got in:
trucks are whirling red
gravel over the roads:
the snow is holding,
packing down: tires aren't
breaking through:

the children, let out of
school, run testing
mounds that look all
snow but are only surfaced,
    scraping up handfuls—
        not yet enough
        snow for
        huge
        crunchy handfuls—

muffled, the highway's
stopped burning:

9:41 pm: we've just come
    in from being out:
it's a wicked white
    icy night:

cars slipping, wheels
        spinning: bushes
sparkle in the headlights:

imagine being out
for a night
restless & wakeful with
cold, some child
coughing—or crying
with fever:

        who are we
        on this globe?
        how & at what cost
        have we survived?

deer & birds:
are they cold?

        maybe one way of
        coming home is
        into silence,

restfulness from words,
freedom from the mill
that grinds
reality into sound:

why do I need to throw
this structure
against the flow
    which I cannot stop?
is there something
unyielding in me that
    can't accept
    the passing away of days
and birds
flowers & leaves?
it's always never return
for them:
that way, day by day, for

me & you:

acquiescence, acceptance:
the silent passage into
the stream, going along,
not holding back:

I try to transfigure these
days
so you'll want to keep
them:
come back to them: from
where?
     from the running honey
     of reality & life?
come back:

I hold these days aloft,
empty boxes
you can exist in: but
when you live in them
you hurry out of your own
life:
          if my meaning is
          to befriend you,
          must I turn you
                    away?

I stop to fasten, and
currents
swirl around, over
me, wearing my
structures away, teaching
me not to grasp, not to
try to keep:

why does a man sit alone
and question
the answerless air where
no blood stirs

and no lips move?

this love, fashioned
    into acts,
    might bring a lonely
    person
    purpose enough:
        what's the nature
of this carrying-on?

generations to come: are
they more precious,
    estimable, than these
    that are?
    can a lip quiver with
    more need
    then than now?

I have a notion to be
wordless, but
    active with immediate
    deed, open
    with the glance of my
    need, direct,
        humble in my going,
glad
as the thoughtless are:

are we creators in fact
or collectors of relics:
    do we make grow
    or cast into stone?

19 Dec:

this ole world could be
        one

                    if it wusn't
for hate
        bustin it apart,
        keeps
        crackin it
into little pieces:

love, I mean, could
        rise up there love
and make all the
children dance
        shaking breasts & hips,
pelvis
shooting in & out
and all kine of sanging
going on:

summer coming back just
like it hadn't been
        nowhere:

and the bees
        bumbling
in the hollyhocks:

calves kicking up their
heels &
the spring roosters
crashing into crows:

in Praxagora's perfect
world, tho,
the maiden could be had
only after the hag
        was served:

and what would we do with
our hate?
turning hate outward, we
keep dense & pure

our inward love:

can we incorporate our
enemies?
can we maintain a high
degree of difference
        within unity's cluster?

give room, latitude, widen
the band
        of acceptance: we live
in strictures of hate
& suspicion, intolerance
        & doubt:

absorb the margins:
enlarge the range:
give life room:

20 Dec:

today is cold: hit
        ten last night:
        and it not winter
        yet:

        the sun comes high
into the room: strikes
the inside wall
three feet up from the
floor:

we're going to Philly tdy:
little more shopping:

7:19 pm: oh it was a cold
        windy day, jaw-tight,
ear-numb, nose-runny, cold

windy day: the sun
        seemed to do no good
        (pigeons hovered
in the morning sun
along the steel trusses
of overpasses) and the
wind burst
from intersections down
the dark street-canyons:
concrete, stone, steel,
hard & cold:

having shopped for hrs,
I sat a
few minutes
in the waiting room (on
        the balcony) at
        Wanamaker's:
(or do they call that
the gallery?):
mostly old folks:
some dozed: the eyes of
some begged
        out of strictures:

the circles of reach:
in the womb, confinement:
then, opening, the
        bassinet: the cradle,
playpen, the house, to
school, enlarging always
the widening circle: then
away to college
or military service, the
        circle so large
        now as to be
        congruent with earth—
the total openness:

then the gradual
shrinking,
stiffening, the star-
brittle bones,
eyes fading,
arm-reach,
        and the last
        confinement:

my, my: & nothing to be
        done:
nothing to be done!
is any time left?
carpe diem, snatch, grab,
hasten, do, jump, go:
    get the rose, da
rose, da rosa baby: see
    that girl? when
    she turns her head

& stands lost, her eyes
blank with something forgot,

universes
crack up into little
    pieces & blow away

    and something quite
    silvery
    starts singing—right

out in public
and whoever said men can't
be blossoms because

        looking at her,
        near her,
        they

bloom warm,
they just rise up,

something liberally
extending itself,
    expanding

and they turn to hot jelly
& freezing little bits
    of ice

and say "God" under their
breaths
and under the burden of
    something too much
    to have or lose:

it's go: go & green:

the day we went to York
    I saw
a black&white cow
    standing close to
    the sunny side of a barn:

animals know a good many
things: they'd
    take over if
    they had hands:

21 Dec:

the jay was out
    before sunrise
wheeling & dealing

& around noon
a covey of quail
    enjoyed (apparently)
    the sunlit margin
between the back lawn

and the sumac grove:

now, at 3:58 pm the
sun is yellow,
coming into its
          horizontal: about
a half hour to go:
they used to say
"half hour sun":
          I used to tell
sun-time, right
out of the burning clock:
have a gold watch, now,
     that takes its heat
from me: times change:

our tree, which I just
put up, was
     "Grown in Canada"
     &
     comes via
     Puyallup, Washington:
the tag says:

22 Dec:

we lost our mule Kate in
the fall
to a chattel mortgage:
     men backed the truck
     up into a shallow
ditch, dropped the ramp,
& with twitch & whip
loaded her on:

it seemed, rather than

            justice,
violation, breakage:
tearing into
a mule's knowledge: &
I stood by, a boy,
violated & hard:

Kate was small, willing
at a touch of straw
to run a wagon harder than
you meant:
        she lunged in the
        high-boarded truck:
her ears flicked, her
eyes set back, blank &
reasonless: she
drowned from herself & us
when the motor, roaring
over all meaning,
tore into gear:

farm with no mule:
the corn she made
    to lie all winter
in a barn's weevil-dust
& rat droppings:

in the spring, a tragic
mule, bony,
        majestical
        came to us:

never forget first time I
saw her, coming down the
Chadbourn road: my
        father went to town
        in the morning:
late that afternoon,
sitting on the washbench,

96

waiting, I saw him
    coming, new wagon &
new mule:
she seemed hardly to be
walking,
but the legs went out &
out in a reach
    that covered ground:

I called her Silver—O
    loved beast,
    dead & gone,
    not to be lost from mind
    & song—
because
though huge & tired, she
wd rise to her hindlegs
at a touch of heels to
her sides
and run stiff & fast: like
the Lone Ranger's horse:
& Silver was black:
    she possessed the
mark of play,
        a liveliness silly,
inappropriate & great:

10:17 pm:
we went to church at 4
this afternoon:
I held a lighted candle
in my hand—as all the
    others did—and helped
sing "Silent Night": the
church lights were doused:
    the preacher lit his
    candle & from his the
    deacons lit theirs &

then the deacons went down
the aisles & gave light to
each row
& the light poured
down the rows &
the singing started:
     though the forces
     have different names
in different places &
times, they are
real forces which we
don't understand:
          I can either believe
          in them or doubt them &
          I believe:

I believe that man is
small
& of short duration in the
great, incomprehensible,
& eternal: I believe
it's necessary to do
good
as we can best define it:
I believe we must
discover & accept the
     terms
     that best testify:
I'm on the side of
whatever the reasons are
     we are here:

     we do the best we can
& it's not enough:

23 Dec:

I was thinking when I woke
up how much more I wanted
ice cream than breakfast:
    the wake-up radio was
saying
the most dread terror is
    fire at sea
(ship burning in the
Atlantic with 800 aboard)
and that forecast for
today was snow, turning
    along the coast into
    sleet & rain:

release us from mental
prisons into the actual
    fact, the mere
    occurrence—the touched,
tasted, heard, seen:
    in the simple event is
    the scope of life:
let's not make up
categories to toss ourselves
around with:
    look: it's snowing:
    without theory
& beyond help:
I accept:
I can react with
    restlessness & quiet
    terror, or with
    fascination &
    delight: I choose the
side of possibility:

the snow's angling

into the sumac thicket:
I see black &
    white, every twig
highlighted: if I were
looking with the snow,
I'd see
all white:

4:48 pm: the vowels are
lifting around here: breve
a is becoming breve *i*:
    "I c'int stind it."

mansion is *minson*: *palace*,
    pillice:
    O Chaucer:

Muse, you're an
eagle in the mind: when
    you fly away
    the air's relaxed
    & empty:

            come back:
maybe you're sick of
        domestic details & long
    for some swept
        transfigurations,
leading, transforming
ideas, details
    lifted into a
    marshaled whirl:

            I had
            decided to
            give up all
            but details:
            decision
is sandhouse without you:

I acknowledge you, am

miserable without you:
come again
and make your will in me:

or are you here now
whipping a tired spirit
the best you can?
I admit
I've shot my load:
but I can't stop: give
   me a second wind:

   it's there, I'm sure
of it, somewhere in the
mind—another valve to
   open:

   let it open &
   fill this tape
   plentifully up: let
the brim break: tear
thru surface tension
to the spring:

the volcano shoots &
rests, gathering: the
man shoots &
   gathers: give me
a continuous, smooth
shooting, rich
uninterrupted flowing:

do you want me to
wrestle & beg, testify
   your absence: I've
   made a long
piece of it:

26 Dec:

today is bright, warm:
supposed to go up to 40:
   ice in shade:
sidewalks & walkways
slippery:

look what small beach
animals have made: a
    ruddy bird
    with curved beak
that turns stones
looking for
small beach animals!

(the consumed sustains the
consuming form)

thought, too, is voracious:
Berenson sd
   the Gothic arch
ground three centuries of
design
into gothic arches: a
    dominant form,
consuming insistence:

(here I'm probably
converting the fine,
       shaped,
    differentiated world
    into
undifferentiated grist)

I devour the sunlight off
     leaves,
the sound out of jet
     engines, I devour

the whistle out of
         the bird,
         bust his
         guts open
         and devour
their churning:
         where is the
         source?

I eat the wind, frilly as
     a nap, off the
     mossbeds: I get down
& close-up consume
the sense of velvet
off green winter moss:

my heart eats the shape of
your face:

tell me, tell one
moorless in the drift
     of broken forms, who is
the conceiver who
will pour this
regurgitated pab
     into the
     transfigured
saucepans, winejars,
breadbaskets, garages,
space stations
of the new time?

you've heard the larva
chew
in the wood?
grit, grit, grit,
metronomic?
tell me—after
     wood's passage through

guts,
who will recall the tree?

  something's cooking in
  this life!
  can you get on to it?
  (will you need to
  be helped off?)

integrations &
  disintegrations:
  nothing that goes in
  comes out the same
& nothing that comes out
has ever been the same
before:

small beach animals make
ruddy turnstones &
wood meat makes larvae:
but where did the
  turnstone
  get the shape
by which he consumes? &
how
the larva
find that special
  form of stridence?

  things are related by
  opposition & similarity:
  but the periphery
  vanishes into nothingness,
  the stabilizer:
    interior-ward
    is the going in & out
    of shape,
      substance running

through shapes of itself,
itself the running:
the container & the
   contained are
         somewhere
contained by the
universal noncontainer:

frogs & snakes
keep the hawk's shrill
   whistle greased!

      thought jails!
      keep us out!

but
if we get too free,
all the way
into unrelated,
fractured sensation,
    call us back, jail,
occasionally
so we can get a good
   night's sleep:

since there are feelings
   (& thoughts) I can't
   express
   through the forms of
   society,
here I make other forms,
play-forms,
to express them through:
that's the center:
maybe you're listing with
hidden passions, too: you
can work
them off through

                    play-shapes, as I
                    do:

                    use mine:
                    get all the good
                    out of them you can:

          clean up:
          you have to take your
          place
          at dinner: make decent
            conversation:

          we have certain forms:
          reality is to accept them
            at face cost & value,
            change them
            at peril
            & if you do change them
            stay awake
          all night
          wondering what worse forms
          will take their place:

          careful how you go fooling
          around with things: or
          like me
          make sure you're
          fooling:
                fooling takes
                instinct off:

          (it's nice to
          have a good, quiet dinner:
          wonderful to sleep,
              the cop on duty—
          better look out
          before you
          get dissatisfied, you may
          be in for a real

gypping)

can I have that virgin?
nope:
why?
she's taken:
who says?
'ciety:
I want her!
sorry:
I can't stand it!
sorry:

better be careful, bub:
ever thought of taking
up a little painting?
        ever been
interested in "expressing"
yourself in words?
        think you'd like it:

jever think of taking up
mountain climbing:
            beautiful sport!
            dangle from
shocking heights, shoot
off at peaks:
like babes!

like cool it: run it
into approved
    channels:
    irrigation
    in reverse: run it off:
lower the pressure
on the dam:

nice hobbies?
stead of making that
married lady with the

biggies,
jever think of making
chairs?
photography is nice:

sing a song for sweet
society: keeps
ballocks in a row,
        where if you can't
have every gal
        still—obey
the rules—
        there's one you can
have
all your own
and nobody can take her
away from
you

or he'll wind up in
court or behine bars:

sat simple:

think you could have one
    of your own
without not having all the
others?

see that man's house?
I want it:
you can't have it:
why can't I?
it ain't yourn:
why?
because:
I'll take it:
you can't:
why can't I?

because:

there *is* a way:
get good marks in
kindergarten &
discipline yourself so
the teacher likes you
& praises you & tells the
whole community how
    wonderful you are:
    & on up through college:
    & don't get in any
    trouble:
& then invent something or
start a business, and if it
fails, start another:
    or work your way up
    through
a corporation: or start
saving early—invest wisely:
someday you may get
        a house very much
        like that one—you
        may be able to buy
that very one
    if your tastes
    haven't changed in
    the meantime:

sheez!

it's called "coming to
    one's senses":

10:15 pm:

it's been a beautiful
day: warmth
made the light

         glossier: the cedars
and firs
stood
sprung into freedom,
snowless:
the windy morning
      moved a trillion
      waves & branches:

streams
ran clear in the gutters
from opaque
ice:
gutters running under
bright skies,
silent,
ripples unpeopled
by raindrops, oiled
ripples of motion:

      energy
released from the sun
made the gutters
      run: a fact,
ordinary & miraculous:
touch over great
distance: the cool melt
      from a vast,
      frying body:

that it's there:
that we're here!
      we, dependent,
helpless, doing the best
      we can:

bacteria multiply by
simple division:
      changeless transmission:

but also
they multiply sexually,
testing conditions
    with mutant
    possibilities:

    we must keep the
    tradition &
    modify it
so we stay resilient to
change:
too traditional is loss of
change: too changing is
loss of meaning & memory:

27 Dec:

today is
        cloudy
        in several ways:
        details of pain,
causes of shivering: but
this must be done:

    it's fairly warm,
tho—speaking now
entirely of the weather:
        may rain:
        could turn cold
enough to snow again
(none of my business)

I saw the jay
before breakfast:
        he looked a little

                    grimy, gray,
          like old blue snow:
                    has had rough

          times lately:
          rough times is ordinary,
                    will not make
                    the news:

          the sun, screened dim by
          clouds, enters the room,
          strikes my typewriter,
                    throws shadow on
                    the wall,
                    just touches
          the flower-tip of a
          crown-of-thorns branch:

          ecology is my word: tag
                    me with that: come
                    in there:
                    you will find yourself
          in a firmless country:
                    centers & peripheries
                    in motion,
                    organic,
                          interrelations!

          that's the door: here's
          the key: come in,
                    celebrant,
                    to one meaning
          that totals my meanings:

                    the circular lichen
                    spotting the tree
          trunk
          is
          like a moral order: there
          is a center

where with threads the
lichen knits in, the
    "holding-on" point
  that gathers stability
  from bark: and there
  is
the outward multiplication
of forms (cells & patterns)
to an unprescribed
periphery
that marks the
moment-to-moment edge
    of growth:

the cougar, big in
    size & appetite,
ranges widely:
      he won't turn
    a square mile
    into desert:
travels out into the
country of his sustenance,
incorporating herds of
deer
within his trails
and how thin
the tissue of his going
is! one month in
  the northwest of his
  range,
  a month in valleys,
    a month at
higher altitudes:
he's adapted to travel:
    it's not in his
    interest
    to exhaust
the deer population, as

it's not our interest
to exhaust the host earth:
        the predator
husbands his prey:

        at the center,
the predatory gathering
of energy done,
the female drops her litter,

new seeds of possibility:
        new animal-plants
        to take root,
        spread out the wide
thin tissue
of life:

tapestries! figures
        overlapping:

        at the dwindling of green
a percentage of
aphids begins to be
born with wings: time

to fly away &
make trials of new centers:

ecology out of balance
turns tilt into
        direction:

when the milkweed
seed
rises into the wind
on down,
the soft beauty
means conquest:

let's establish ourselves,
send out our tokens:

         as I am I
         I will change you,
drop seeds of myself
in your ground:
watch out for me:
I mean to prevail:

you think of yourself:
    I may welcome some
    thought of yours: I
    may give it ground:
         or I may not yield
         to it: I may find
it lacking,
   not able to survive
   my country,
   & cast it out
   as
   already withered
in potentiality:

the plains Indians centered
their lives
on the chase: rooted in
   a moving herd
   of buffalo!
   a center
stabilized
in instability:

   or the reverse: the
barnacle
on a rock, stationary,
   depends on the sea
to bring it food:

where is the center
   that holds?
   it was the Earth,

became the sun, then
the center of our
galaxy (Sagittarius?)
    then farther &
    farther out:
    no
imaginable center: except
the one
the lichen makes:

my other word is
    provisional:
    we'll talk about that
    someday,
    tho you may guess
the meanings from *ecology:*

don't establish the
    boundaries
    first,
    the squares, triangles,
    boxes
    of preconceived
    possibility,
    and then
    pour
    life into them, trimming
off left-over edges,
ending potential:
    let centers
    proliferate
    from
self-justifying motions!

the box can't bend
without breaking:
    but the center-arising
    form
    adapts, tests the

peripheries, draws in,
finds a new factor,
utilizes a new method,
   gains a new foothold,
responds to inner & outer
change:

28 Dec:

today
is dim
again:

the sun makes diffuse
shadows
that go
in & out
of focus:

         (just now, the
   thorns
   are black
   against the wall)

maybe it's gonna clear off:
not very cold:

there comes the exactness
again:
pulsing:

gaits:
short/quick-stepping Kate:
Silver,
   long & languorous:
   what

to do in case of fall-out:

put it
back in & use
     shorter strokes:

     brushstrokes:
     short, straight, narrow
strokes
that blend & move
     into vague scenes:
     the broad, long
swash of color:

     the paroxysmic:
     the full, slow
inner & outer reach:

     wavelengths:
     distance, elapse of time
from crest to crest, from
point of highest
     stirred feeling
to highest point: the
     silky, fiery
considerations
     down the hills
     and shallows and up
     the rises
         of repeating motions:

rhythm, pace:
Silver, majestical,
     slow but sure: the
     turn-plow
     turned earth
     to overturning rivers:
smooth, rockless,
alluvial country,
     free of stumps:

     stump-holes, tho—still

in the pasture: the
   hollow shells—inside
   the crater lake
   of ancient wood-ambered
rain, wriggling larvae,
hanging head-down from
   the surface,
    breathing through
their tails, & tiny green
frogs
hidden in crevices
over canyons of wood:
   the thick, grazed
carpet grass
smooth in patches
   around inedible
   wire-grass clumps:

worlds:
the only longleaf pine
left
stood tall & spare-boughed
as land-corner:
   marker between
neighbor & us:
mystical tree:
   half ours,
half his, neither
able to take his half
   without loss of all

& in addition
transfigured by
   boundary-meaning,
   entered in the record
    (history in the
courthouse)
a sign:

spared: let us take on

119

meanings to
keep us:

standing alone in the
edge of the pasture,
near the road
(the road when it came
through
cut off a sliver of the
neighbor's land
so it was worthless to
him—our pasture
fence included his
sliver &
the tree stood in from the
road—is the way it really
was: and the road &
tree became symbols
of two kinds of truth,
competing:
the tree, ideals of
truth:
the road, the use of
this world
& compromise)
high sparse
branches
sang
thin songs:
(one of my uncles, I
heard said, used to
go into the woods to pray,
always to a
particular tree:
a praying tree—
must have had
meanings

in it)

if you don't think
mechanisms work
 in the green
 becoming
 of
 the
 lichen, I don't care
what you think: it's
one-sided,
unaware that
 crystals, even,
 exist
 as fluids:

 thallopyte & green
 alga
 living together,
 with
 necessary exchanges:

 abstraction may
 sight far
 over the facts
 & fall
 short or broken
but meantime it shows
saliences of going:
 its spare thin
 beauty
 is relating:

 reason & feeling
 living together, with
 necessary exchanges:

guidelines—but readiness
to adjust

to changed
environments:

what is it that persists
through generations,
    throwing its pattern
    ahead?

    an earth-product,
I don't represent
all my wills:
    others, not mine, are
    in me:

        still, when the
        feelings are working
        right, knowledge
        is redundant: one
        doesn't analyze
        the good
            condition: one
            accepts,
without consciously
accepting, and enjoys:
            let's
            reach out
            from this
            loneliness with
            as much love as
            we can:
            grief is on us:
            we're not
            just right:
            we are hurled
            away by
            exaggeration:

    line us up!
    that's our directed,

122

undirected, or misdirected
wish:
give us an earth
between these frozen poles:

gates:
entrances: doorways:
     wombs:

outward gates: exits:
     broken walls,
bridged rivers & fallen
mountains:

          give us the being
whole
     wherever we are:
     intellect has
cast
     temporary resolutions:
     pity—it's not
     all intellect's fault—
     that now we see
     breakage
     (fragmentation & high
     entropy)

     but
     high entropy
is not loss of pattern:
we can't see:

          the man who feels good
has a shortage of
     problems:
     he's cabbage-cool
& -sweet:

          we must—since
there's only one universe—
bear the tearing up

before we can enjoy the
putting together,
the adjusted putting
               together
          that gives us
          fuller touch
          of what we know:

tho the crust
floats with under- &
    over-seas, it's hard
    as rock

    & anchorages
    in motion are
solider than rock:
    rock wears:
    motion is the full
openness of possibility:

    our existence is
               evidence
               of more
than we can imagine: much
we can't see
is working right:
          let's celebrate
          that part of our
          ignorance
          & keep on
till we learn better how to
praise:

               will you leave
               the Lord
               & sit down
in a man-made misery?
then
you've postulated a lot

for yourself
& lost:

that we're going is
reason to be going on:
(the dance
& warm red dry wine!)

dance! you splendid
    creatures!
       your heel-strings

sing like plucked
instruments!
    your skirts whirl
    worlds
    with inner secrets!

swing!
your partner,
promenade (and when
        you can
        get laid
        get laid)
first to the right, then
to the left, right, left

      (get lawfully
      laid)

    Muse, no mortal
    can have
    enough of you:
he wants bigger &
bigger draughts: he wants
to get drunk on
    and in you:
he wants to consume you:

can you stand to be
nibbled on, Parnassus, by

a million nibblers?
　　wonder there's any
　　chance I could
　　chew off a big
　　hunk of you?
　　　　　would you
　　　　　mind
　　　　　more than
　　　　　the
　　　　　tickle of
　　　　　tiny
　　　　　teeth?
from the gouge I made in
you
would gush springs up,
too, Pierian,
　　bread washed down
　　with wine:

(better confine myself
to steak)

　　the immortal body
　　replenishes itself,
the constant banquet:

so they did eat & drink:

and you keep giving me
juice,
I may drive through
　　all this
　　raillery
　　& come on
the vine-water of truth,
the slot
　　of hazeless sight:

and you give me the ole
steam, baby,

126

I may get all these
gargoyles up,
  lined around the high
  edges,
  and then you may give
  me
  two or three columns
  & a plain wall:

and I can keep bringing this
stuff up,
  every fool thing
  shining in
  the light of its
  foolishness,
    I may get
    cleaned out
good,
worthy to taste your
simple fare:

oh wash all the crap out!
I want to tremble with
need
when I reach for yr bread:
  let lust for yr wine
  parch my tongue
  so
the bread sticks:
  I hate hungering
  & thirsting,
  yet will I
  hunger & thirst
and go to the foot
of the table,
  pinch crumbs
  off the floor—if you
will grant me

wide arm-reach
    & lifted
    voice
    so the table shakes
    & the people enter
the maze of yr presence!

        come on, now, f'god's
sake, what're you saving
it for?

                the light
reclines:
of a brightness not yet
gold: white gold:
    Bach runs in his high
    rant
    from the record
        player:
        we're going
        out
        to dinner:

30 Dec:

today is 19 &
    sunny:
    the still-warm tide
    comes in
    &
the shallowing marshes
freeze & keep it:
    increments of
    continental shelf:
    ocean loss:

we may sink:

    the gulls fly inland
looking:
     the dump swarms with
     gulls & smoke:

    yesterday I gave
to the memory of

   William Carlos Williams

    (reception in NY
for Mrs. Williams)
     sat in the back of
     the bus up
& the motor ground my
head to dust (gray,
     graphitic)
     & a man fell
in a fit
in the bus station: three
men held him till
he jerked still:
     a crowd circled &
     watched:

(we're monkeys, scratching
our heads
& asses &
dumb with joy & tragedy)

    so many people
with bodies only:
     so many bldgs with
     mere addresses:
     buses, subways, cabs,
somebody everywhere:

fragments: faces never to

be seen again: isolations:

poets, peaks of need,
    loose cold
    majesties,
sizing heights, cut off
from the common
stabilizing ground of their
admirers:

        peaks relate across
        thin
        &
        icy air:

        how good to be back
        here
with ruin's blue-bottle fly,
whole fields wasted with
grass,
an empty cherry tree
& one jay:
        sunlight on the wall
        with precise
        black thorn:

5 pm:

        some rosy drifts
        still in
the west:
        are the days
        gathering moments at
the edges?

          every moment
          of light
          nudges
          my cold

rhododendron &

every inch
of this rising tape
    ruffles my blood
for the gathered product,

the heaping hamper,
accomplished florescence

                empty places
                make room
                for
                silence to
                gather:

            high-falutin
            language does not
            rest on the
            cold water
            all night
            by
            the luminous
            birches:

            is too vivid
            for the eyes
            of pigeons,
            heads tucked
            under wings in
            first
patches of sunlight:

is too noisy to
endure
the sleep of buds,
the holding in
of the huckleberry
blossom:

too voracious

                    to spin,
                rest
                & change:

                is too clever
                for the frank
                honey-drop
                        of the lily-pistil:

                        I hear the
                        porkchops frying!
                        ah,
                there's the sweet, burnt
                smell!
                        sounds in the kitchen,
                        pots lifted
                        with empty
                hushing ring,
                the plunger of the icebox
                        door
                        snapping loose: the
                        sizzling roil of
                        porkchops turned:
                        protest, response:

                        flashes of aluminum
                light
                        as the pots work, the
                        glint of tines
                                as the table
                                dresses: the
                                holy
                                slow
                                lifting & turning
                in the spinach pot:
                rituals, hungers,

                        motions over
                        fire,

the stance &
tending:

   I hear & visualize
   & the drop
under the tongue
bulbs clear
& pressing:

what's that sound?
mashed potatoes being
    whipped?
    there, a chop turned:
    cups winding up
still in saucers:

  the grasping snip of
  celery stalks:
  the high whir of
the garbage disposer,
chewed clear:
    a rough, troubled sound
    now
    of another charge, maybe
    the grapefruit rinds:

        "You
          can
          come
         sit
          down
         now
        if
         you
         want
        to."

  6:08 pm:

    no vegetables at all:

133

(the grapefruit I had
       earlier—is that
       a vegetable?) we had
porkchops & rice &
       a salad (pecans, raisins,
apples, celery, lettuce):

so wonderful to be just
the outside edge of
       painfully full:
       then coffee!

I wish my words could
  be quiet
  as if
waiting for a mt to
dissolve:

  or for a burnt woods
  to make
cones and acorns:

just north of here's
the pine-barrens—maybe
       30 x 50 miles:
hasn't been underwater
since the Miocene,
       when it was an
       island: has a
       fern
       found
nowhere else in the world:
and a fox there
has a modified kidney:

all around deciduous
forests
took over the rising land
so that's why
the barrens

is still an island
        (botanical):

    our woods, mostly
    scrub oak
    & pine,
    have three levels:

    the lowgrowth of
    floor shrubs:

    then laurel,
Quercus marylandicus, and
tall shrubs:

    then oak & pine:

    pine used to be
    dominant here: but
when pine is cut
oak takes its place:
    when oak is burned
    over, it
    sprouts,
five- and six-trunked:
determined:

one day last summer I was
driving long the road
over by Gravelly Run an I
    seen this turtle
    just going
    in the bushes: so
I stopped (because my
            nephew loves'em)
and when I stooped to pick
up the turtle,
I seen a sight: his back
    was hazy with
    mosquitoes, thick

as they could
    stick,
bumming a, now mind you,
ride on a turtle's back!
    saving their wings
    & certain
sometime they'd be
brought to water:
    didn't see anything
like that in NY:
    economy, full use
    of possibility:

            (if you were
                sitting on a
                    distant strand,
        longing for home,
        you'd have to
        conjure up things to
        occupy the time,
        too)

            9:15 pm:
            but is it
            possible to
            talk the chaff
            away? can
windy vowels
brush off all the bits of
paper
& leave a clean place for
    the simple design?

    screens
between us & memories
    we can't bear:
        what unmentionables
of guilt & terror!
go back & see

terror as fantasy,
guilt as innocence?

    but we've
    purposely lost
    the road back:
take it on
faith
we knew no better
then, did the best we
could,
    & are repentant
    for wrongs
imagined or real:
instinct protects us:
let's accept this
provided & open
    possibility & go
ahead:
we may redeem ourselves:

feelings, troublesome,
  volcanic:
  disturbances held
down, deep as control
can reach:

should we let go a little?
is it our fear of feeling
  & not feeling itself
that pours concrete slabs
across our lives?
    can we open a valve
& let ourselves go
flat like a tire?
    or must we have that
pressure for our riding?

11:15 pm: my wife says if

you put soft
cookies with
crisp cookies the
crisp cookies turn soft:

bad apples with
good apples: bad
potatoes with good
potatoes:
(2nd Law Thrmdnmcs)
soilage spreads
&
nature is trying to get
everything back
into the mill:

we exist because we're
afire (& burning out):

31 Dec:

today the dry burn in
my nose of a cold
coming on:
I should have known:
that bus back
from NY the
other night
had no heat—I'd put my
coat in the rack—and the
guy beside me fell asleep:
(he woke up in pain:
had had a few
beers
before boarding the bus—
said

they were the longest miles
he'd ever ridden: express,
    sir, we don't make
    stops)

little girl ahead of me
kept trying to push her
seat back, hitting me
    in the long-legged
    knees:
she waited till I seemed
asleep: then, ram! wow:

people:

her mother, beside her
in the aisle seat, was
rather attractive:
scratched her daughter's
head: daughter said, that
    feels good: & scratched
    her mother's head:
    (grooming: no lice
    to pop in teeth as
            reward)

energy transformations:
how do
porkchops make
my body turn?

energy, conserved, weaves
in & out (perhaps not
    as a
    separation—structure
    & function
    are
    inextricably
    intertwined) is
stored, released,

transformed—
    still continuum:

  what is the
subcellular machine
in the eye that
converts
radiant to electrical
    energy?
    in the chloroplast,
radiant to chemical
    energy?
    how do fireflies
    turn
    chemical into
    radiant energy?
    the nerve,
chemical
into electrical energy?

mechanisms: necessary
    exchanges:
    worked out & perfected
    (proved
    practical) long
before we stood
by the shores of
incredibly ancient sea:

if we looked only by
what we know,
    we couldn't turn our
    heads:
    if we were at the
    mercy of what
we understand,
our eyes couldn't see:

    discovery is

praise &
understanding is
celebration:
but understanding
    is to see itself
    fallen short:

our proud words
        (that possibly
            tear & defame what
        is)—why
    we don't know
    how porkchops
    give us the mouth!

        but speech
        potential was
there
& we realized it: we
speak:
    cabbage
    releases energy in us
    that trembles
    our vocal cords
to tangle with air
& give it shape!

        Lord, I'm in your
hands: I surrender:
        it's your will
        & not mine:
        you give me
        singing shape
& you turn me to dust:

undefined &
indefinable, you're
        beyond reach:

what form should my

praise take?
   this long thin
   song?
   to be
simply & completely
human?
    to unite
    everything that has
    been made
     with
     tenderness?

    we've made
     miracles of our own!
    spaceships
abstract as the laws of
motion:
    the pure design of
    wooden bowls:
     wonders & matters
of fact: but

where did everything that
   is
come from?

    while we can't
understand, we can
feel
and
that's a fine essence,
astonishing as the
mitochondrion—
     if
     not
     more
     so:

leave structure
to the Maker

& praise
by functioning:

1:26 pm:

    I feel a little
    shivery:
    the cold's making—
forgive me—headway:
but I just had a baked ham
sandwich, glass of milk &
coffee,
    that to be
    transformed into
    whatever ammunition
    it can:

    after this,
this long poem, I hope I
can do short rich hard
    lyrics: lines
    that can incubate
slowly
then fall into
symmetrical tangles:
    lines that can be
gone over (and over)
till they sing with
pre-established rightness:

    here, I plug on:
    whatever the Muse
    gives, I release
for
this is one possible kind
of song
& has one kind of veracity:

    I've been
    looking for a level

of language
that could take in all
kinds of matter
& move easily with
    light or heavy burden:
    a level
that could,
without fracturing, rise
    & fall
        with conception &
        intensity:
        not be completely
outfaced
by the prosaic
& not be inadequate
    to the surges:

    I've hated at times the
self-conscious POEM:
    I've wanted to bend
    more, burrowing
with flexible path
into the common life
    & commonplace:

    the denominator
here may be too low: the
lines may be
too light, the song
    too hard to hear:
    still, it's not been
    easy: it's
    cost me plenty:

last day of the year:
I've been at this
    25 days—this
idle tendance
of typewriter & Muse—

nearly a month of Sundays:
    I'll miss the
    hovering over time,
the watchfulness—an idea
about to take hold,
an image reach for shape:
    I'll miss the
gathering up into days:
but not all art runs
along: it sometimes
    stands by,
    selects, stores,
alters,
hardens till
    like a boulder it
nearly halts the running on:

I anticipate: the
empty tape is still
    imposing,
    frightening:
    the unconscious will
have to act out
several more shows
before the marginal red
ink
warns it's time
    for a new tape:

poetry has
one subject, impermanence,
which it presents
with as much permanence as
possible:

the moon was I suppose full
last night:
it cast exact shadows:
  9 degrees this morning

with the highest
atmospheric pressure
recorded since 1927:
    something like 30.82
    and mostly sunny
    today:
    clabbering up now
(3:50) though:
thank it's agonna snow
some:
don't keer if it do:

memories, tapestries:
a huge
    wild cherry tree
    grew
    in the bank
    of the old deep ditch
    that cut
    all across the farm
    from road to swamp:
     field-tree, shady
& cool: big roots, turned
gnarled as bark,
stuck out deep down,
dark
with damp:
vines o vines
  running here & there all
  over the place tangling—
  jasmine vines or some
kind of honeysuckle
(not the shrub honeysuckle
of open woods)
     but deep down in the
     ditch, crawled into,
     an opening, cool,
vineless,

with somber trickle of
clear water:
that's where I used to
        find the
        diamondback
turtle: yellow stars on
black shell: cool &
                mysterious,
with ruddy-yellow spotted
mouth: a hold of
        wildness
            leaping in the veins—
like a fountain, or,
prolonged, excitement
        moderate & lingering
as a spring
oozing into the ditch:

        a full tree, alone,
that took on space far &
high as it could reach:
    corn wdn't grow
    anywhere around:
    would yellow,
shrivel, never come
to tassel:

    that's why
    one May
    we girdled
        the tree, a narrow
belt of white meat
showing and then
the old heavy branches
lightened
        and all the stiff
        fingers
        pierced black pleas

into the empty sky:

in my memory all is
white with blossom: the
ground is
purple with
blackcherry stain:
 and green
 leaves hold
way up into the day
an oasis of cool,
 settling air:
 the turtle swims
in my hand:
water nearly declares its
running on:

times so far gone: a
new nakedness
 at the ends of rows:
 a new nakedness
 of need:

how can these
pictures stay
in my head:
 how, after lying 30
yrs in darkness, can
they be brought up,
looked at, and
resubstantiated?
 what we don't
 know's a scare:
 & comfort:
how could we react
if we heard the machinery
of our reactions?

 there is a silence

in us:

            here
            I
            will
            make
            room
            for
            more:

the record the surf leaves
on the shore
        relates tenuously to
        any given wave

        yet is an exact
        history:

                I can't hear
                all the waves
                lapping
                back in my life
                still
                there's a song
running through,
wanting to come out here:

        country darkness:
no street-corner light:
a yellow kerosene
lamp
across the fields, blown
out:
        stars
        in an uncompromised
clarity
rush into, dusting
        the heavens:
        see that?
        where?

over there—cat-eyes:
two little stars:
look at that
luminous dust,
the thick axis of the
galaxy:
on
this cool
sandpath
I'm experiencing
the galaxy?

human concern in
country darkness is
narrow
& short of range
in a wide
rangeless house!

1 Jan:

raining:
at the borderline &
promise
of snow:
gale warnings up
along the coast:
no small craft to
enter heavy water:

(the gulls are safe:
on the ground, they stand
erect into the wind
that divides from
the beak around them:

in the air—why, the
wind can't harm what's
on the wing)

    too much stability
can't prepare
for the day
  resilience is the style:
  go up with the wind,
fall sideways,
    wings taut to balance,
into the wind:
handling
(winging) what disturbs,
use of & victory over:

took down the tree:
undressed it:
    stripped off
    bright red
& frosted yellow balls
    & blue bells: unwaved
draping ropes of tinsel:
lines of twinkle-lights
  falling straight from
a top circle
like bars in a hoop,
  disbranched:

  heaved it,
stiff, shriven, out the
back door
into the rain:

    silly tree:
    lying there, shorn
of meaning, some
strips of tinsel
glistering

with sorrow of old joys:

        an old woman
glittering
with jewels &
   timeless paint:

beauty that's been used
   can't comprehend
the special contempt
   of loss: lifts its
   wrinkled chin
   & lets
tears dance,
   held in a stubborn
   survival of will:

        or
        maybe
        the tree,
naked,
caught with a ragged
    glitter on,
welcomes
   the return of its own
   dead
   branches
to their natural
configuration
     and loves the cold
     beading
     & hanging on
of rain,
in that remnant truth,
alive:

or maybe
knew
better than the beholders

and even at the moment
of its highest shining
a perishing
that drove rain
among its ornament:

      (I forgot what
       I was going to write
       about today)

(it was going to start out
something like—wise up,
you guys)

have I prettified the
    tragedies,
        the irrecoverable
        losses: have I
glossed over the
unmistakable evils:
has panic
    tried to make a flower:

    then, hope distorts
    me:
    turns wishes into lies:

I care about the statement
of fact:
    the true picture
    has a beauty higher
    than Beauty:

minds
that have made so much
    effort,
    learned all over
    again
the alphabets,
    the battles,

153

architectures,
vegetables,
monarchs,
philosophies—
minds
unique with memories,
of conversations,
bodies,
homesteads,

degenerate, wear thin,
wear out,
and the woven,
worked fabric
disperses:
the fragments
lose meaning:
the light
that was on each fragment
goes out:

I know
the standing on loose
ground:
I know the
violence, grief, guilt,
despair, absurdity:
the sky's raw:
the star
refuses our wish,
obliterates us with
permanence,
scope of its
coming & going:

I know what it is
to feel around in
the dark
for a hold

& to touch
nothing:

we must bear
the dark edges of
our awareness:

taken in our measure,
   we're unexcelled:
      perceptions:
appetites & satiations:
beside the terror-ridden
   homeless man
         wandering through
         a universe of horror
dwells
the man at ease
      in a universe
      of light:

      let's tend our
      feelings &
      leave the Lord
      His problems
         (if any): He
got us this far on His own:
& millions have come
& gone in joy
   (predominantly):

2 Jan:

today
feels above freezing & is
sunshiny: so
   bright on the tape, I

squint,
inhibited & frustrated:

don't want to close the
blinds: three plants
in here
(besides the
crown-of-thorns): they'll
use the sun
soon as it moves over
a little:

   feels good on my back:
I thought I'd thrown off
that cold yesterday (plenty
      of grapefruit
      & water)
but I feel stuffy again
this morning:
ragged vocal cords:

the soul accepts areas of
reality
that are machineries to
      gratification: income,
praise, sexual pleasure:
      but when the areas
      return
frustration &
loss of self-esteem, the
soul shrinks back into
detachment, cold &
      uncommitted:

      no one questions
      pleasure or the
      reality of its
      source:

mazes here: shifts,

compensations, balances,
impositions, demands,
dislocations, exchanges:
    working together,
out, & against:
some areas clearing into
resolution:

one fellow says, get
money: the wealthy are
excused: wealth, in a
        hard world, is
        proof:

        another says, do
what you're here
to do: money's
    secondary:

        success or failure:
terms of definition:
another fellow says,
    be successful:

when authority is
    multiple &
self-contradictory, look
inside,
formulate & defend
your own authority:
    many different sets
of things can work out
right:

they say creation is
thwarted unless
a man accepts & realizes
himself, stands open
& finished

as a flower:

what of the evil man?
is he evil because he
realized himself
or because he didn't?

conflict between
self-realization &
society:
   how's the adjustment
   to work out?
   can society cut its
individuals down? can it,
without crumbling, bend
to accommodate them?

complicated, inconclusive,
organic,
working itself out: so
the center,
   strongly rooted,
is rooted in motion:
a nexus
always becoming, its
      strength
      relatedness:

poured into an axiomatic
box
one pays the cost of his
security:
   (may be a fair
   buy—depends)

earth holds in motion
      by poise
      between gravity
      & centrifugal
force:

           the lichen's safe
with the tree:
the tree lasts a long
           time in the earth:
           the ground
keeps still:

motion holds us
apart, related:

I send this ahead:
    can you
    take a liking
to the song?

when we meet,
           will you shake hands,
           offer me a drink?
will you tell me
how you're moved by
fears & dreams & what
           your plans are
           & exactly
what you think about
when you wake up at night?

if I seem aloof
will you spot it as a
           guard
           & help me down? if I
           act insincere,
will you know it's my fear
you will expel me from
           your sincerity?

           see the roads I've
           traveled
           to come to you:
           monsters I've engaged:

           have I earned the grace

of your touch?

and if I sit blank,
   hearing the high
      conversation of
the Muse, listening
hard
to get the words right,
will you understand
I've not scorned you?
   and if the song she
   gives,
pressing in its naked
insistence, repels you,
will you
still allow me to serve
   one
higher than your praise
or blame?
   will you care for me
   specially because of
   that?
can you tolerate another
woman in the house?

high in the mid-forties:
mostly sunny & mild:

   quantum physics
   in human affairs:
      the laws work
      about the same
in bodies, morals, or
politics (or art)
   but
   the law
   you can't pin down is
   the one coming:

   ancient laws with

the built-in
possibility of novelty:

    fellow said
    everybody says "when my
    ship comes in"
    says
"they never sent one out"
    one smart cookie:
says his ships return now
from so many directions
      he can't keep up:
      &
      every
      one
      loaded
      with
      money:

      pure
      money:

the economic forecast will
increase his fleet
if it comes true:

thirty yrs ago he didn't
have nothing:
now there's nothing he
    can't have:
        (can't have the
        thirty yrs back,
        but neither can
            you)—
trouble is, he says, if
you can buy something you
don't want it:

doesn't want anything &
has a million bucks to

prove it:

he sacrificed & sent the
ships out:
    I think he's glad:
    he's a glad,
independent man: loves
a lot of inexpensive
things—bushes, roses,
    maypops:
       loves them with
       complete ease,
not having to run
somewhere to do something:
apologize he
should be working: unh-unh:
    talks with you in
    detail
    about rosehips (home-
       grown)
    as if nothing else in
    the world mattered:

I know another man who
worked just as hard,
spent every dime and now
is old & in a kind
of rant:

    don't ask me what you
    should do:
    if you decide to
sacrifice, you'll
do the sacrificing—&
there're no guarantees:
it's your business:
    figure it out
    for yourself:

    if you don't look out

for yourself, who else
has the time?

11:10 pm:

    the eleven o'clock news
says
the plane that went down
in the early December
storm
was hit by lightning:
    the pilot said
something like, "This is
flight 214: we are
going down in flames":
& the tower said something
like,
"Flight 214: we have
your message":

3 Jan:

today is warm & sunny:
may go up to 50:
    the light seems
to have body,
& the crown-of-thorns
that lost nearly all
its leaves is
  sprouting green tips
along the branches:

(one way of standing aside
from the fight
  is to win it:
failure's more despised

than cruelty)

      my cold's worse:
      in the chest:
      feel puffed &
      weak: but
gotta keep moving along:
it's impossible
there's not an end to this
tape:
      move along, little
dogies:
Wyoming must be somewhere:
don't throw your heads
back to lick
shoulder flies:
don't put that front leg
out
      & bend to graze:
      git on, for God's sake:
      that mountain's
been ahead three days:

      the sun strikes my
      coffee & puts
a ring of light, like
Saturn, on the wall:
two poles
with bobbing center:
jiggling design:

      (the conservation of
      angular momentum:
      transfers of energy
of motion:
there're many levels &
at some of them
      abstraction works:

like a charm)

the vine that (still
     green) tangles under
     the cherry tree
reminds me of a brain:
why?
it's a vine:
or of a bed of sexual
   nerves
   intermingling:
             or it's the
             held green,
the durable freshness, of
what keeps low,
      undercover
      (cherry tree & sumac
             grove): or
it reminds me how
reality can go so many
      ways
      at so many levels
& still keep the "roundness'
   of a clump:
      discernible unity:
but it's vine:
   I put mirrors in it
   & behold myself:

      given mind, we became
strangers here:
with mind, we convert
   strangeness
      to humanness:
      we unnaturalize:

4 Jan:

3:20 pm: today is near-
ly shot aready:
   got up ear-
ly & drove
mother- & father-in-law to
Philly for train to Fla:
Phyllis & Mary came, too:

stopped on way back at
Korvette's & traded in two
records Phyllis gave me
for Christmas—Elizabethan
& Jacobean songs: ugh:
   I got 3 of Bach's
   cantatas instead:
somebody may have written
music before
or after Bach but
it wasn't necessary:

& I like all kines of
     music:

        the day
       dwindles
       down:
   warm again:
    mid-fifties:
gladioli blades up,
scorched at the edges:
when came they up?
   warm spell first part
of Dec:
   too tall—5″—to've
   sprung up in couple

days:

an ant reconnoitering
the kitchen counter:
    is't that hot?
    & a squirrel out:

the fool sayeth there is
no God
    because he can't tell
    what He is:
the wise man sayeth there is
a God
    because he can't tell
    what He is:

    there's unity,
but objects don't
describe it:
nor do words:

if you go east on an
east-west highway
    this time of year
you will find dirty
snow
on the right (by woods)
and a sunny bank (by
woods) on the left:
    the reason is,
with the sun low south,
the trees
turn their shadows
on one side:
    that's a fact:
    caught up
in an abstract
    configuration:

a further reason is, the

highway's wider
than the length
    of the shadows:
    wouldn't work with
footpaths or woods roads:
the proposition is:
when the width of the
highway exceeds the length
of the tree shadows (depends
      on the kind of
      forest — sequoias
      would require a
      vast
thoroughfare) then one
roadbank will be
sunny
(providing it isn't cloudy)
          :

    or night:
        :

    unless there's
    a moon:
        :

      in which case
      it would be
      moony: etc:

    now, predict
yourself some things with
high probability:

of course, it must have
snowed:
& mostly melted:

5 Jan:

today is sunny & it may
be warm again:
        the jay was in
        the cherry
tree
breastward to the sun &
he jumped up & opened his
underwings
        to the warmth,
        looped & flew away:

        went to dinner last
        night (jayless)
at Copsey's
        with Tom & Mary
        & we all
had lobster tails:
feller said was the best
tail he ever had anywhere:

program & comment in most
music:
        not
        in
        Bach
        or
        Mozart:
there, the clear-cut
lofty
motions of musical forms:
no knights thundering
through woods, as in Mahler:
no mania cross-country-in-
the-clouds
of Beethoven's Ninth:
    in Bach & Mozart

the meanings are
detached, exist among
themselves:
emotion lifts
to intellectual feeling:

without abstraction,
fact is
meaningless with isolation:
    but abstraction by
the loss of fact
is "out of this world":

6 Jan:

today is splennid again:
    sunny as to leave no
    clouds to be excused:
    how I coughed
through black time-gaps
    & time-emergences
    last night:
        red-eyed & indoors
        today:

    coming home:
through spotted round
    stones with
    egg-careful feet:
    through thornbrush
    across emery sand:

    who was that I was?
    who's that from
    rumblings, dark baffles,
    trying to

break, overriding,
        into song?

give me some imago I can't
become:
        steadfast in the
        unrealizable:

when we solve, we're
saved by deeper problems:
        definition is death:
            the final box:
hermetic seal:

relieve our hunger, then,
for forms:
        give us the
inexhaustible feed: the
box is full outside:

(a drop forms at the
icicle-tip, tapers, pulls
free, rounds-up (slightly
flattened falling-side)

breaks free (little
        explosion of fact)—
the precise event
    (sometimes audible)
when it hits the ground)

        jever watch a leaf
        trying to turn over?
            one edge may be
caught
by the projection of a
stonelette
from hard ground:
the wind
whiffs

and the free edge lifts:
falls back:
trembles a little
  in steady, low wind:
    gusts way up,
     nearly vertical,
nearly flop-overable,
but falls back—
  oops, caught
    still at a
45-degree angle
by a sheet of steady,
      higher wind (higher
  than the low):

the action seems no way
intended to satisfy
you—that is, complete
itself
by flopping over:
  sometimes after hours
  of agonizing
  expectancy,
the wind,
suddenly & inexplicably,
will die down:

    maybe, it'll be
rain finally that turns
the leaf over
or floats it off its
    hang-up:
    or a
  completely
  unanticipated deer
may step
right next to it
& so disorder the ground

as to shift the
stonelette
1/64″ away: so should a
wind rise
then
why the leaf would have
time to gain momentum
before it struck the
hang
& so, whirling,
somersaulting,
    wd vault right over:

    but the leaf may
    jam &
    leap free all in a
        second!
breathlessly satisfying:
nature's entertaining
but makes no effort:
go thru life: some things
    you see, some you don't:

they told me the
small world was concrete,
    inexhaustible, & where
        to dwell:
        so I dwelt there:
        & went smaller &
smaller till
everything turned into a
    wave-particle
    dilemma:
nothing to hold, taste,
hear, or see:

11:08 pm:

    day exhausts:

          night renews:

forms of thought
please or terrify, but
tire:
    the mind
    in its strife
for completion
pales, blurs, dries &
    crinkles up:
    sleep turns
    another way: to the
spring: what's the source
of that fresh water?
how
does it come up into our
days?

7 Jan:

today is rainy:
started around 7 last nite:
a quiet
    warm rain,
musical in the gutterspouts:
    I woke up a lot
coughing last night
and my awareness would
break into
the rain's-song—a segment of
    consciousness—right on
key & phrase: rain's never
out of tune: a ragged
range of sound, small &
large events, assuming

a low, bell-like
resonance:
    random averaging
into clusters of random:

there's a blur-shadow of
sun:
it's clearing up:
the window edges on the
wall are sharpening:
what's going to happen?
no, the blur dies:
the window disappears from
the wall:
    not now, not yet:

two jays in the sumac
    grove: they make
        no patterns:
as would three or four:
from branch to ground
to cherry tree
    to lawn: always two
    poles
of an invisible world,
shrinking, enlarging,
dipping, twisting its
            axis:
two points of radiation:
    two sources
with magnetic field:
close in
and the emotions rise—
    anger
    or affection—
and then one jay flies
away:

even so, the magnetic
lines hang
with tenuous hold:

sometimes you can keep
track
of the patterns five birds
make in a woods edge or
    open tree:

    beyond that,
you start to have the
large round
    congregations,
individuals
lost to the general
    symmetry:

random flocks with overall
    direction:

facts are that way: more
than a few
& the facts are lost
    in a round hypothesis:
    while one fact
    or two,
though surprising & concrete,
can't make a meaning:

another haze of sun
and a quail calls from the
    field:

only the lively use of
    language lives:
    can live
    on dead words
        & falsehood: the

truths poetry creates
   die with
   their language:
     stir any old
language up,
feel the fire in it &
its truths come true
   again:
   the resource, the
creation, and the end of
   poetry is
   language: the
mead-mad bard
did not
depend
on nuclear physics for his
   song,
   but on mead & word:

other elements are:
1) isolated perception
2) related perception
3) imagination: word &
     image in surprise
4) transfiguration
5) dream: ego &
     transfiguration

& there's feeling,
   invisible matrix: &
music!
    the going tension
      that holds us,
suspends, rises & falls,
the going on:

poetry is art & is
   artificial: but it
realizes reality's

potentials:

Channel 12 (NET) just gave
    this list of common
    nouns, with plurals:

quarrel	quarrels
shelf	shelves
study	studies
donkey	donkeys
canary	canaries
goose	geese
speech	speeches
knife	knives
ditch	ditches
deer	deer

    hear the sounds,
note the ir-
regularities, the vagrancies
& rules:
a language is a particular
instrument
with possibilities
peculiar to itself: bring
    out the facts:
    utilize & heighten
them into untranslatable
sound:

which is the other element:
    (the substance of
music: tho music is an
    integration higher than
    pure sound—oriented
    into waves)

poetry has no use, except
this entertaining play:
    passion is

vulgar when not swept up
into the cool control
of syllables:

sorrow is brown & empty
unless
ocean vowels thunder
        from it in
organizations like surf:

then is sorrow that never
was,
come in an ocean
        that cannot reproduce
        itself:

11:10 a.m:
        the sun's bright
        through the window:
hits the right side of
the thornbush,
        illuminating half a
        dozen
        green leaves:

        they'll make food
& pass it around
to limbs that got no sun
today:

thornbush island: sits
        in an old
        triangular ashtray
          in a red round
          ceramic pot:

ashtray sits on a dry rug:
        removes from nature
        & the sweet ground:

in the pot, a soil,

179

reticular with roots:

add water
    &
leaves sprout:
blossoms blossom:
    where's the living part
that transfigures this?

under the rug is a mat:
under the mat is
oak floor & subfloor:
under the floor is
    7 feet of space
    &
    under that
12 inches of concrete
and under
that
the ground:

      o island!

        how distant you
        are
        from the true hold!

(& earth will send out
seed
in self-sufficient ships,
beading
space with possibilities—
what a separation)

      (somewhere
       they
       may
       take
       hold
       again!)

how many levels of drought

& stone
have I put
between
my soil & flower?

poetry's my
false water, black
    soil,
            dry blossom:

get out of boxes, hard
forms of mind:
go deep:
penetrate
to the true spring:
            give up
            these islands:
(they're safely apart —
    but apart:
    take the risk of
    moving in)
merge with coming &
    going common life:
    drink
    the average
        drink:

the system apart, complete:
    add water
    & serve the bloom:

    bloom that doesn't
    come to seed,
no need throughout the
    rooms
    answering the need:

2:18 pm: didn't
    stay sunny long:
    say it may

rain again: but then
tonight clear off
& turn cold:

8 Jan:

today is sunny & warming:
last night the temperature
must have dropped lower
than the predicted 30:
    because yesterday's
    rainpools were
    frozen half an
inch deep this morning:
(see where the tires broke
through)
        sunny & cheerless:
no mail (as usual) at the
box: three requests
for subscriptions from
magazines: thrown out
unopened:

lonely, isolated business:
since what one sez or duz
    means nothing, one is
free to sa & du
what one likes: nobody
    will get very jarred or
    pleased: one
acquires the
indifference & moderation
of neglect:
    it's out of order to
    be passionate with

concrete:
    or try to lift a
water-spiral from the sea:
turn in anguish, scream
    & sprout leaves of song
        & generally work up
            a good deal of
    dust—the placid
world returns
cool sky & glassy
            concern: what
            must I do
            to reach
            the top?

        something else:

years ago, I had a way of
thinking about
truth (again):
    how to determine the
    topography of
the ocean's floor:
soundings: one here,
one there: a sample
depth of an area wide as
a steel cable:
    the more soundings,
    the more clearly (& truly)
the stippled terrain
    begins to appear:

soundings twenty miles
apart
will approximate reality:
    (tho you could miss
    a fabulous cleft
    or cone):

only infinite (impossible)

samplings could
produce a map symbolic
of the truth: & then the
map would be too small,
every sounding translated
   into a different
   dimension:

the only representation
of the sea's floor
is the sea's floor itself:

  we take soundings & we
get schemas, approximations,
but we can't come
to the whole truth:

  then I'd turn the method
to the mind, make soundings
on & on, get some vague
stippled configurations:

realized the mind can't be
rendered up:
  say what you please
(or I please) about me:
it's partial
  & schematic: I'm
  free
  &
  unknown:
  the only me that is
is the me that is:
tho there are
organizations,
saliences, directions
  approximately
  perceivable & reliable:

long as we can't exhaust

ourselves, we can
grow & change:

1:31 pm:

unity & diversity: how
to have both: must:
   it's Coleridge's
   definition of a poem:

   somewhere, far off,
things come together,
hope rising from and
     moderating strength:
     somewhere, far off,
there's no expense to the
part
in the whole:
    somewhere
the ideal, the abstraction,
takes on flesh:

what a celebration! our
little earth
united, shining in peace,
   hate managed,
   rerouted:
   the direction thru
   history is clear:
unity amassing larger
& larger territories,
    till now
neighborhoods of nations
meet
under the name "United
             Nations":
    the cost has been
    great in
time & slaughter, it seems

we've already earned
the prize:
    let it be:

    these are the
motions: listen to
their music: improve
    their economies:
atoms make molecules &
molecules make
    matter & matter
makes a universe: go
that way:
rise:
    rather than
    abolish the
particle (individual)
unity, strong, self-assured,
may afford the
    individual
    more comfortably than
    division could:

7:38 pm:

    deep down inside are
    fireworks
    & a whole mess of rivers:
    very interesting
    country:
rip-roaring violences &
someone solicitous
    fanning an angry one
    in the shade:
        one over by a rock
        making up songs
as if there were no
world at all:

186

a wiry, fur-ragged lecher
    running with
    lawless hard-on,
whickering, leering, &
licking his lips:
        one
writhes, a beautiful lady
    with high
    feathery hat
doing a spike-heeled dance
on his heart,
tossed clear
into the merciless open:
        two squabble,
vicious geese,
rending each other with
verbal knives
of disappointment:
& one,
prisoned by contrary
        winds, sits rigid,
distant:
            two
            young lovers
give & receive, fall
asleep, wake into
mysteries, no world
beyond their reach, no
    further completion:

I'm afraid to visit:
    wd take another tape to
get there: & reliable
trip ticket &
return ticket in advance:
& a lot of
time to think it over:

thinking's safer:
(not as much fun, prhps:)

***

a man's center is his
woman,
  the dark, warm hole
    to which he brings
his meaning,
offering & receiving:
other meanings take
wider orbits: many orbits
  of meaning:
    that's the nucleus:

you been lookin for a
center to the universe?
's it:

            11:06 pm:
  was out by
the refuge
again this afternoon:
  froze up:
  birds gone:
  cept Canada geese:

  they were
waterborne
at a melting edge along a
bank:
  I scared'em out
    & they
slipped & skidded on the
ice! threw their wings
  out
    to right themselves
    with air:

  two bald iggles

been sighted out
there:
tell me:
can you beat that?
  I looked for any but
couldn't find some:

9 Jan:

today ben
    der clouds
downwashen
        die rainingdroppes
        und
tickleticklen
der puddlepoolens

        und
all around ben der wind
upswelling
    und sideswashing
        dem glitterglassen
windowpanen:

und smalle foules haben
der tails
downgedroppen
        for offdrippen
der raingingdroppes:
und die upshouten mouths
    ben upshuten gehaben:

    Muse, let
    my blood
stir!
    and, you, hear

189

arteries & veins
bring song
bridging heart to heart:

the tenderspoken
assurer: the gentle
    enlightener &,
till enlightened,
    protector: arrive:
    say you're
    going on a journey
& need one to teach:
teach me,
father:
    behold one whose
    fears
    are the harnessed
    mares of his going!
fiery delights,
    pounding hoof
    & crystal eye:
    where before
    dread
    & plug-mule
        plodded:

clod:
mere earth:

    how the cornroots
    lift
    earth out of the
ground:
clod,
I'll infuse you
    with blood:
    show how many ways you
    can be
unlike a clod:

quiver with incredible
    fire—oh, burn,
      transfigured sod!—
squeeze
your slick cold hands
in the fear
& pleading of death:
      clods are
      dispassionate, come
in geometries &
configurations most
beautiful—you, tho,
    with how much
    ferocity,
what violence of outrage,
can you defend your
woman?
unto a clod, how unlike:
dance!
    throw in:
    throw yourself
      into the river
      of going:
where the banks also flow:

      yesterday at
      the refuge:
red hawk,
sprung up from dike reeds,
in each claw
   held
   a shoulder-wing of a
    robin-size
    bird,
the parts clinging
together, empty spaces,
threads, the raked,

ragged body:

I don't know what
Canada geese think:

they see the
little bird
fly by
under the hawk
        (last
          flight—
the ground covered unseen:
the feather-molding
    wind unfelt,
cold air
rushing in
where a heart was,
        rushing
        through
where was
back muscle of wingbone)

                        ***

tho you have wronged me,
still I love you:
        (that ought to put
          the squeeze on you
          good)
                (see you get out
                  of that one):

don't do anything specially
moral: I may want to
shed you:
        wrong me:
        with the wrongs you
do me, I unlock myself
from the prison

of your tenderness:

    the clean fight
    in bed
    turns
    into children!

    I will consume
    you: consume
        me:

I break away
into my gratified self:
leave me alone:
don't smother me with
    unrequited concern:

    you cushion &
    absorb my thrust!
    be a wall, for my sake!
    resist
    so I can plunge you
    down:
        this soft way
        unmans me:

        ah, but sweet
        rest, that pliable
        wall
surrendered, loose:
that hairy stone
rocking with my given
        pool!

    who are you?
    come out in the open:
    let me see you:

your breasts, the
pellets

afloat in warm white seas:

    I will eat your
    mouth:
    crush the
    numb of love
    out of my
    lips:

who are you I have not
figured you out: you
    shift: you're here
    & there:
    changing, yielding,
    presenting;

    stand in one place:
    let me anchor
    my connection: do
not fight me to death
by swimming
away, side to side:
    don't drive me crazy:
    be still:
    the ache possesses
    me:

    let's fight it out:

turn this strife &
    celebration
        into infants:
        there's the warless
        love,
the giving that receives:

Muse, provide:
    entangle me beyond sense
or need of place:
    let me far & richly in

so
the words pour:

we have yet a while
to fill this tape: it's
getting small:
it turns fast:
    before long
    the red edge will
    rise
from the floor: it'll
climb,
go under the roller, then
turn up
& out into the light:

how glad I'll be then!
I'm so tired
you can't imagine:
I want to do other things:

    and you, O supposed
(& actual maybe)
reader: how
weary you are!
I've bludgeoned you
with every form of
    emptiness: you've
    endured my
    wrestling need:
    may something accrue
to satisfy you:

let's sit down & exchange
tenderness of speech:
have I deserved the
    engagement of your eyes?
    may I take your
    time?

this noise & length
says
I honor your moments
of silent understanding:
let's sit down on
a parkbench
   & talk how the world
appears & disappears,
sung through
by light we have the
tune to:

if you find me
dropped in a corner
   from the circles of
   conversation,
   come in continuous
motion, without breakage
of barriers,
& confer the touch of yr
speech upon my lips:
   I'll reward you
   with secrets of
   hands &
dandelions, money-needles
& moonlit nights: the
   weeds
   have given me
   their bitter song:

   come with need
   to a specialist
   in need:
   we'll exchange
   gaps,
     fulfilling:
      our spaces will
      let us

                    come close:
                    intermingle:

if suddenly I
  get up
  & blow the joint—
I haven't forgotten you:
    don't think it for a
    moment: please:
sometimes, when I'm
off-balance &
unsuspecting, the
Muse takes my mind:
      if I'm not to lose it
      & her
      I have to follow,
clear out in a hurry:

      at another time,
      you'd be surprised
      how much I can
      remember & care:

der greyische skies ben
    maken
    sidewalkens
        into mirrorshiners
mit mistyfoggendroppes:

10 Jan:

today is windy as March
& sunny:
        a window whines like
boring bees:
        the outside lid

of the exhaust fan
in the kitchen
flaps:
the wind's muffled weight
falls against the end of
the house:
whipping branches
    in whistling trees:

    we turn away from
    galaxies
to the warm knot
in the dark:

    somehow in taking
    pleasure
        from yr body,
    I have given you
    my heart:
    I care now
    more for you than for
    the pleasure you give
    me:
        you, your total
self, my anchorage:
the universe shifts its
center:
it turns about you:
    who are you?
    will you destroy
    me?

    went to a
    party last
    night:
    & the living room was
    large:
    the guests sat around
the walls

in a periphery of beads:
some beads clustered into
groups:
    but it was too far
    to cast a line
    across the room's
vacant center:
lack of unity:
disintegration overall
  with random
  integrations:

    fun, tho: beads
shift,
regrouping the periphery:
combinations:

my plants are in full sun
now,
the chloroplasts
  are working round the
  peripheries of cells:

        look!
        there's the red
        ink!
        rising from the
        floor:

Muse, I've done the best
I could:
  sometimes you ran out
  on me
  & sometimes I ran out
  on you:

    I know you better now:
    you've come closer:
      will you
      confer the high

grace of your touch?
come & live enduring with
me:
       I'll be faithful:
       I won't trick you:
       I'll give you all
       I've got:
       bestow tendance &
concern:

help me to surrender
myself:
       I'll be the
       fingers & keys
of your song:
       I'll ask nothing
       but the sound
of yr voice:

reader, we've been thru
a lot together:
       who are you?
       where will you go
       now?

           ***

coughed a lot last night:
round
4:20 a.m. got up &
   took a shot of
   brandy:
   numbed the tickle
some:
   slept better:

   just had lunch:
cold baked ham:
coffee: chocolate fudge

200

cookie:

   last night had duck
(Bobby's favorite) at
Mary's: conversation:
        hearing people
talk, how marvelous:
I'm alone too much: get
to think
other people
     aren't people:

the 200-inch glass
shows a
billion-billion galaxies:
what is God
   to this grain of sand:

   dispersions:
   it's as brave to accept
boundaries,
turn to the center given,
& do the best you can:

     think of other
     people: devise some
     way of living
     together:

get some fun out of life:

how about the one who sez:
  it's too late
  for me to start: I
  haven't got anywhere:
  I can't get anywhere:

    how do the hopeless
    get some fun out of
    life?

    apes get

something out of life:
they don't ask what is:
                bamboo shoots,
tender, cool:
they have a head man:
    they pair off
    & raise babies:
    they defend:
    they sometimes rest in

clearings
and groom themselves
    in sunlight:

have our minds taken us too
far, out of nature, out of
complete acceptance?

we haven't remembered our
bodies:
    let's touch, patiently,
    thoroughly: beyond
    vanity:

but for all our trouble
with the mind,
look what it's done:
    a fact at a time:
    a little here (there's
the red ink
turned into the light!)
a little there:
let's be patient: much
remains
to be known: there may
come
re-evaluation:
        if we don't have
        the truth, we've

shed
thousands of errors:

haven't seen the
jay:
a sparrowhawk
can stand still
in a high wind, too:

coming home:
how does one come
home:

self-acceptance:
reconciliation,
a way of
going along with this
world as it is:

nothing ideal: not as
you'd have it:
testing, feeling the way:
ready to
readjust, to make
amends:

self, not as you would
have it:
nevertheless, take
it:
do the best you
can with it:

I wrote about these
days
the way life gave them:
I didn't know
beforehand what I
wd write,
whether I'd meet

anything new: I
showed that I'm sometimes
blank & abstract,
sometimes blessed with
song: sometimes
silly, vapid, serious,
angry, despairing:
    ideally, I'd
    be like a short poem:
    that's a fine way
    to be: a poem at a
time: but all day
life itself is bending,
weaving, changing,
adapting, failing,
    succeeding:

    I've given
you my
emptiness: it may
not be unlike
    your emptiness:
    in voyages, there
    are wide reaches
    of water
    with no islands:

I've given you the
interstices: the
    space between
    electrons:
    I've given you
    the dull days
when turning & turning
revealed nothing:
I've given you the
sky,
uninterrupted by moon,

bird, or cloud:
        I've given
you long
uninteresting walks
so you could experience
vacancy:

old castles, carnivals,
ditchbanks,
    bridges, ponds,
        steel mills,
        cities: so many
interesting tours:

the roll has lifted
from the floor &
our journey is done:
thank you
for coming: thank
you for coming along:

the sun's bright:
the wind rocks the
    naked trees:
    so long: